Hindu Gods Goddesses:

Spiritual and Scientfic Approach

Hindu Gods Goddesses:

Spiritual and Scientfic Approach

by

Pandit Harendr Upadhyay

PILGRIMS

PILGRIMS PUBLISHING

◆ Varanasi ◆

Hindu Gods Goddesses: Spiritual and Scientfic Approach
Pandit Harendr Upadhyay (Jyotishratna)

Published by:
PILGRIMS PUBLISHING

B 27/98 A-8, Nawabganj Road
Durga Kund, Varanasi-221010, India
Tel: 91-542-2314060
E-mail: pilgrims@satyam.net.in
Website: www.pilgrimsbooks.com

Edited by Christopher N Burchett
Layout & Cover design by Asha Mishra

ISBN: 81-7769-268-2

Printed in India at Pilgrim Press Pvt. Ltd. Lalpur Varanasi

DEDICATION

To, The Lotus Feet of Lord Shiva The Master of Universe this book is dedicated with reverence

Kali Bhakt

Pandit Harendr Upadhyay (Jyotishratna)

Specialist in both Eastern and Western traditions of Astrology, Palmistry, Phrenology and Tantra-Mantra

CONTENTS

ILLUSTRATIONS

SCHEME OF TRANSLITERATION

Vowels		*Consonants*			
अ	a	क	k	त	t
आ	ā	ख	kh	थ	th
इ	i	ग	g	द	d
ई	ī	घ	gh	ध	dh
उ	u	ङ	ṅ	न	n
ऊ	ū	च	c	प	p
ऋ	ṛ	छ	ch	फ	ph
ॠ	Ṛ	ज	j	ब	b
ऌ	ḷ	झ	jh	भ	bh
ॡ	Ḷ	ञ	ñ	म	m
ए	e	ट	ṭ	य	y
ऐ	ai	ठ	ṭh	र	r
ओ	o	ड	ḍ	ल	l
औ	au	ढ	ḍh	व	v
		ण	ṇ	श	ś
				ष	ṣ
				स	s
				ह	h

श्र śra क्ष kṣa ज्ञ jña त्र tra

Visarga (:) ḥ Anusvār (.) ṁ

FOREWORD

How and wherefrom this boundless cosmos came into being, is the eternal query that has been disturbing human mind from time immemorial. The Vedic response to this query is as follows:

In the beginning, only Hiraṇyagarbha was there. He was the only master of the entire creation. He held the cosmos all by himself and only he deserves our worship.[1] There was a Supreme Being in the beginning. From His mind, the Moon came into being. From His eyes the Sun arose. Vāyu (air) and Prāṇa arose from His ears and fire was born from His mouth.2 From the naval of this Divine Being arose the mid-sky (Antarikṣa). From His head arose the uppermost sky (Dyuh). From His feet arose the earth and the ten directions assumed their being from His ears. Thus the cosmos was materialised by the Supreme Being from different parts of His body.3 From the Supreme Being all beings arise; they live in Him and ultimately are dissolved in Him.4 From the Supreme Being, sky came into being. From the sky, Vāyu was born. From Vāyu emerged fire. Fire led to the birth of water. Water resulted in the birth of earth and lastly from the earth arose vegetables and creatures.5 The entire manifestation emerges from the abstract

---

[1]Ṛgveda – 10-121-1

[2]Shukla Yajurveda, Puruṣa Sūktam – 31-12

[3]Rgveda – 10-90-14

[4]Taittiriya Upaniṣad – 3-1

[5]Taittiriya Upaniṣad – 2-1

Supreme Being in the day-process. As the right-process sets in, the entire manifestation is dissolved in the Supreme Being which is abstract, invisible and intangible.6 In fact, the entire manifestation is incomplete by itself; it is dependent on the Supreme Being for its entity, movements and acts. For example, the Sun appears as shining but it does not shine by itself. So are the moon and the stars; they do not shed their own light. Similar is the case of lightening and fire. The light they shed is not theirs. Everywhere, it is the light of the Supreme Being. He is the ultimate source of light. It is the light of the Supreme Being that pervades through the entire manifested cosmos. In other words, the Supreme Being sprays light through the suns, the stars, the moons, the lightening and the fire.7 This is Vedic cosmology.

The foregoing exposition of Vedic cosmology may be conceptualised as a circle whose nucleus is the Supreme Being and the rest of the circle is the manifested cosmos. The manifested cosmos arises from the nucleus in the emergence course and merges in the same in the reverse course. The two courses are *ad infinitum.*

Cosmic circle is run by three deities, Brahmā, Viṣṇu and Śiva. Brahmā creates all the creatures on behalf of the Supreme Being. Viṣṇu maintains the creatures. Śiva's role is dissolution. The dissolution is not a negative role; it is a pre-condition for regeneration. Śiva sits on the confluence of dissolution and regeneration. This is His uniqueness. He is unique on one more point. Whereas Brahmā and Viṣṇu have only male figures, Śiva is half-male and half-female. He is called *ardhanāriswara.* Brahmā, Viṣṇu and Śiva are Vedic deities. The other prominent Vedic deity is Indra. In the praise of Indra, ṛṣis have composed

---

[6]Shri Mad Bhagwadgeeta – 8-18

[7]Mundakopaniṣad – 2-2-10.

maximum number of hymns. In the Vedic text, Indra is depicted as the most powerful deity. He is deemed as the deity of deities. Varuṇ, the deity of water also occupies a very prominent place in the Vedic text. In addition to these manlike deities, natural items such as fire, dawn, air, sun, moon, earth, sky, rain, and soma have also been depicted as deities. Fire is a very important deity in the Vedic text as it carries *āhuti* to the devtas offered in the Yajñás.

The Supreme Being reincarnates Himself for the regeneration of mankind, to arrest the degeneration of morality and to uphold the regeneration of *dharma*. He physically appears on the earth from age to age. Major incarnations of the Supreme Being are *Kurma* (tortoise), *Matsya* (fish), *Vārāha* (boar), *Hayagreeva, Vāman, Nṛsimha* (half-man-half-lion), *Paraśurām*, *Rāma*, *Kṛṣṇa*, *Buddha* and *Kalki*. The Kalki incarnation is yet to take place.

Out of the above mentioned incarnations, two, namely Paraśurām and Rāma are contemporary. Rāma and Kṛṣṇa incarnations of the Supreme Being have made a deep imprint on man's mind. The incarnation of Viṣṇu in the form of Buddha created a new wave of compassion and love in the heart of man. Buddha was opposed to any kind of violence against any living being—man, animal or other creatures.

But the incarnation of Viṣṇu is a rare event. It does not occur very often. To check man from his day-to-day deviations and violation of moral code, spirits of several deities are lodged in his organism. In all, there are fourteen deities lodged in the human body to enlighten man as to his proper course of action. The Sun resides in man's eyes to provide vision to him for the right action. Aswinīkumārs keep watch on the nasal activities of man. Man feels the presence of Dik (directions) in his ears. The presiding deity of mind is moon. Let it be mentioned that the moon is born from the mind of the Supreme Being i.e. Brahmā. Viṣṇu watches the movement of each and every human being by his presence in his feet. The deity called Prajāpatī resides in the genitals of man. Human body is rendered sacred by the presence of so many deities. In addition to the above body-dwelling deities, there are several other deities which though not residing in the human body, affect the same immensely. A short description of such deities is given below:

(A) Kāmadeva is the deity of sexual passion. It is a deity without form. Kāmadeva was burnt to death by Lord Śiva as the former tried to trap the latter under his grip. Later, Lord Śiva felt pity on Kāmadeva and granted him eternal life sans body. (B) Yama is the deity of death. Yama rewards the virtuous and punishes the wrong doers. (C) Bhairava is the incarnation of Lord Śiva. (D) Gaṇeśa is the son of Lord Śiva. He is elephant-headed. He is a deity who drives away ill omen and blesses man with boons. (E) Kārtikeya is the son of Lord Śiva. His vehicle is the peacock. Vehicle of his brother Gaṇeśa is mouse. Śiva's family is an example of arch enemies living together in amity. The peacock's prey is the serpent and the serpent eats mice. This family spreads the message of peace through its life-style. (F) Hanumān is the most worshipped deity of the day. He is the incarnation of Lord Śiva. His father's name was Kesari. His mother's name was Anjanī. He was the only fighter and soldier of Rama's army who remained with him till his departure to his heavenly abode. (G) Balrāma was the elder brother of Lord Kṛṣṇa. His weapon was the plough. It is because of his weapon that he is called Haldhara (holder of plough). (H) Dhanawantarī was a great physician. He emerged from the churning of ocean. (I) Nārada is eternal traveller and singer on Vīṇā. He was the mental son of Brahmā. (J) Kubera is the deity of wealth. He was the elder brother of Rāvaṇa. (K) Viśwakarmā is the mythical sculptor, who has magical power of constructing buildings.

Above is a short description of male deities. Along with male deities, there are female deities who if worshipped with genuine devotion bring peace and happiness to the worshipper concerned. The female deities are considered to be the primeval source of energy. Even Rama had to propitiate female energy to win the war against Rāvaṇa. Durgā in an extreme spurt of anger trampled Lord Śiva under her feet. Her vehicle is the lion. She is said to be lion-mounter. She killed many demons like Śumbha, Niśumbha, Mahiṣasura and several others. As she has nine forms, she is also called Navadurgā. Other female deities are Gangā river, earth, cow, Gāyatrī Mantra, Rādhā, Pārvatī, Sītā, Rati, Swāhā and Swadhā. Swāhā symbolises the energy of ignition. She is the consort of Agni. She presides over Yajñas. Swadhā is the presiding deity of Srāddha.

Vedic society is hierarchical in nature. On the top of social hierarchy stands the Brāhmin Varṇa. On the base of the hierarchy lies the Shudra Varṇa. The mid-strata belonged to the Kṣatriya and Vaiśya Varṇas. The hierarchy was originally functional which later degenerated into factional. Individual life in Vedic society was divided into four stages each of twenty-five years. The first is Brahmacarya stage. It is the learning stage. In the second stage, called Gṛhastha, the individual marries, earns and begets progenies. In the third stage, he prepares himself for retirement from family life. This is called Vānaprastha. The fourth or the final stage is Sannyāsa. At this stage, man breaks all ties with his family and exclusively devotes himself for liberation from the earthly bondage.

In the course of his life on the earth, man is rewarded for his virtuous deeds and punished for his deviations and misdeeds. Some divine law rewards and punishes man. This law is invisible. This is called the Law of Karma. According to this law, one must reap the results of one's good and bad deeds.

Man does not live by bread alone. His search for the unifying principle underlying the immanent reality goes on but this principle cannot be visualised by physical senses. Ṛṣis were gifted with inner vision. Through their inner eyes, they identified this principle and revealed the same to the common man. As Ṛṣis could not share their experiences with the common man in ordinary language, they resorted to symbolism. Let us illustrate this point with the help of an example. The Ṛṣis came across a mystical syllable called OM. This cosmic syllable permeating the entire creation could not directly be communicated to the people confined to the sensual vision. So, Ṛṣis evolved the symbol of OM for the benefit of common man. The other synonym of this symbol is praṇava.

Śruti posits that essentially there is no difference between Ātman and Parmātman. But in the actual practice, the Atman identifies himself with the body wherein he is lodged. So the barrier called body makes the whole difference. His potential energy lies buried in his corporeal system in the form of a serpent called Kuṇḍalinī and elevates himself to the peak of spiritual ascendance. Ṛṣis called it hath-yoga. There are seven plexuses (Cakras) in the human body. The lowest Cakra is called Mulādhāra and the apex is Sahasrāra. Man's target is Sahasrāra. Through sādhanā, he awakens his Kuṇḍalinī in slumber and renders it upward-oriented. The awakened Kuṇḍalinī breaks the five mid-way Cakrās and reaches Sahasrāra, the ultimate point of evolution. The moment Kuṇḍalinī touches Sahasrāra, the Sādhaka is transformed into Śiva from the body confined Ātman.

Yogic exercise culminates in the evolution of spiritual feeling as mentioned above. Access to deities is possible only through the identification with the same. One should worship deity by being deity himself (*Devo Bhūtwā Devam Yajeta*). Worship of deity does not yield the desired results till the worshipper identifies himself with the same. Seen from this angle, baseless queries in respect of deities by persons sunk in worldly web are meaningless.

The entire Nature has been trifurcated into *sacred (Divya) profane (Adivya)* and mixture of these two attributes

(*Divy*ādivya). Man's and the deity's basic propensities are profane, and sacred respectively. In the event of deity assuming human figure, his/her personality degenerates into the mixture of the two propensities. It is a scientific fact that Nature's evolution moves from low to high. The profane Nature constantly struggles to grow into sacred. Through this process the profane Nature gets transformed into sacred and thus the duality is transformed into unity. This, in short is the basic theme of the concept of deitiness. Numberless souls continue to evolve from lower to higher level through a Divinely Ordained scheme. As such, there arises a possibility of countless sacred souls. The process of evolution leads individual soul from the state of duality or diversity to the ultimate state of unity or monism. The worshipper and worshipped grow into one. There remains no difference there-between. This in fact, is the perception of the unity in eternity.

Worship of any deity amounts to the worship of the ultimate deity or the Supreme Reality called *Brahmn.* This creation is filled with all sorts of deities, which ultimately merge into Brahmn (Sarva *Devamayī Sṛṣṭiḥ Brahmaṇyewa Pralīyate*). This is the Vedantic theory of Creation. If man projects deitiness in every thing, animate, inanimate, he attains the right of assuming the sacred form. Deity worship differs with the variation in the worship-process, worship-method and the nature of deity concerned. Scriptures declare that deities are countless (*Anantā* vai Devāḥ). This means countless people can worship countless deities in their own countless ways.

Pt. Harendr Upadhyay perceives unity in diversity and *vice versa*. He has thoroughly studied the nature of countless deities as described in the Hindu scriptures. On the basis of his deep knowledge, he has presented a scientific portrayal of the deities. His efforts are really praise-worthy and commendable. That this book would dispel all ignorance related to deities, is my conviction and hope. I further hope that other scholars would emulate Pt. Harendr Upadhyay in writing such books with a view to enlighten the path of materialism-blinded people of today. Here and there some errors may be located in the book which is quite natural, keeping in view the fact that to err is after all, human. I, full-throatedly congratulate Pt. Harendr Upadhyay on his brilliant piece of work on a theme which, to the best of my knowledge, is unprecedented at least in the English language. This is a unique work on Hindu deities in many respects.

SHIVJI UPADHYAY
PRO-VICE-CHANCELLOR
Sampurnanand Sanskrit University,
Varanasi

ACKNOWLEDGEMENT

My most reverend great grandfather Late Pt. Nand Kumar Upadhyay was a wonderful scholar and devotee of Astrology and Tantra. In his shadow respected grandfather Late Pt. Maha Dev Upadhyay followed in his foot-prints. Respected father Pt. Suresh Upadhyay is following the same tradition. It is the result of their blessings that I have been successful in writing this book. I pay my humble reverence to their worshipful feet again and again.

Before writing this book I made contact with several scholars. I got great help from them in solving my problems. I have no words to express my gratitude to Prof. V. M. Shukla, former Vice-Chancellor, Gorakhpur University. Professor, Tribhuwan University, Kathmandu, Nepal, Professor and Head of Chemistry Dept., (BHU) and president, Indian council of chemistry, who helped me come into close contact with learned and renowned scholars of Varanasi.

I am much indebted to my unique friend Shri Anand Mishra; Respected Dr. M.S. Pandey (Professor Deptt. of English, BHU); Epitome of humility and wisdom Dr. Mahendra Pratap Mishra (Lecturer in English, Rukmini V.I. College, Baijnattha, Varanasi), Renowned scholar Dr. Banshi Dhar Tripathi (Ex-Professor, Deptt. of Sociology, M.G. Kashi Vidhyapeeth) and President – award – winner Dr. Murali Dhar Pandey (Professor, Rashtriya Sanskrit Vidyapeeth, Jammu) for their guidance, suggestions and encouragement.

I want to express my special reverence to the embodiment of wisdom and simplicity, my well wisher respected Shri Sheo

Shankar Mishra, an able editor of Hindi magazines and books, who has helped me in many ways in solving the problems in writing this book. It will be ingratitude, if I forget to express my thanks to Prof. Achyut Ram Bhandari, Tribhuwan Univesrsity, Kathmandu. Basant Ballabh Bhatta (Geeta Press), Shri Ram Nihor Yadav for their active contribution and Pt. Param Hans Mishra, Chief Secretary, Shri Bharat Dharma Mahamandal, Varanasi, author of many books on Tantra. Also Anant Shri Vibhūshita Jyotish and Sharda Peethādhishwar Jagatguru Shankarāchārya Swami Swaroopanandji Maharaj has blessed me by writing his benediction. May my reverence to his feet remain the same for ever! I wish to express my reverence and thanks to Dr. Swami Prapannacharya, member of Raj Parishad standing committee, Kathmandu Nepal.

I can never forget the generosity of the most reverend Prof., Shivji Upadhyay (Pro-Vice-Chancellor, Sampurnānand Sanskrit University, Varanasi) who has encouraged a new writer like me by writing the foreword. Also S. Pranam Singh (P.G. in Painting, Vishwabharati, Shanti Niketan) Head of the Dept., Painting, BHU, who made available the portraits for the book.

I have no hesitation in confessing that this book would have not been published if the above mentioned scholars had not helped and blessed me. Therefore I pay my respects to all of them once again.

In the publication of this book some foreigners have also encouraged me by sending their good wishes. Among them some remarkable persons are Marc Burckhardt (Switzerland), Hiromimasuda (Tokyo, Japan), Lee Alan Perry (U.S.A.) Ginamarie Penningion (California) and Martin Seller (France).

Pt. Harendr Upadhyay

PREFACE

Indian scholars have divided knowledge into three parts, *Ādhyātmik* (ontological), *Ādhidaivik* (related to gods and goddesses) and *ādhibhautik* (material). In the literature of other societies, plenty material is available on the three points. But Vedic exposition on these points is far more clear and explicit as compared to the same elsewhere. This fact has been acknowledged by the philosophers and thinkers all over the world. It is said that a single man's life is inadequate for the study of hymns and philosophical books authored by the ancient Vedic scholars. For example, the *Gītā* is a small book consisting of seven hundred verses. It has been translated into several languages. Yet the mysteries of this book remain as undeciphered as ever. Indian literature enshrines vast knowledge both spiritual as well as scientific. It is very difficult to identify and explain such a vast content of the Indian literature. In the present book, out of the three sub-streams of knowledge mentioned above, I have concentrated on the one namely *Ādhidaivik*. The word *Ādhidaivik* consists of two parts namely *ādhi* and *daiva*. The two words jointly produce a new meaning. In short, in this branch of knowledge our ṛṣis concentrate on deities—their names, their shapes, their hands holding weapons, their dress, their colour, their musical instruments and several other such things.

India is full of diversities in respect of climate, language, seasons, caste, living-beings, vegetation, and bodily structure. Similarly, diversity in colour, weaponry, mouth organs of deities is also found. One naturally grows curious to know why a deity's face is elephant-like, why another deity has six faces; why yet another deity has horse-like faces. What is the mystery behind a deity having four or sixteen arms? Why a heavy-bodied deity opts for a small vehicle like mouse? The mouse being the vehicle of Gaṇeśa. What does all this mean? Why Jagdambā (the mother of the world), a compassionate deity opts for the lion as her vehicle? Sarasvatī (the deity of learning) mounts on goose. Mahādeva opts for the bull as his vehicle. What does it really mean? In the Purāṇās, there are details of the colour, shape, vehicle, food, and the weapons of deities. But, why is it so? There is no definite answer to these queries in the Purāṇās. Here and there no doubt, short answers of these questions are found but details are not available.

To find out the answers of such queries, I have spent nearly fifteen years of my precious life. I read several books on the topic in several languages including English and have brought out the spiritual and the scientific answers of the queries raised above.

The book has been written with the object of presenting the pantheon of Hindu Deities in an interesting and understandable manner. Thus this book includes a Devī Section, a (Matri section), a Deva section, (Pitri section), a Veda Deva section, and a Purāṇa Deva section. In the Matri section, primeval female energy, her well-known figures such as Nava Durgā, Nava Gaurī, Sapta Śatī, and seven Ghrita mantrās have been discussed. The following is the detailed description of the first section (Devi or Matrikā section):

1. Nav Durgā, Śailputrī; Brahmacāriṇī, Candra Ghaṇṭā, Kūṣmāṇḍā, Skandamātā, Kātyāyinī, Kālarātri, Mahāgaurī, and Siddhamātā. Also the description of Durgā is found In Tantrik literature. The following are the Durgās of Tantrik literature. Neelkaṇṭhī, Kṣemakarī, Harsiddhī, Rudrānśā, Van Agnī, Jayā, Vindhyavāsinī, Rūpmāri.

2. Navgaurī–Mukhnirmālikā, Jyeṣṭhā, Saubhāgya, Śringāra, Viśālākṣī, Lalitā, Bhavānī, Maṅgalā, Mahālakṣmī.
3. Saptamātrikā Gaurī-Brāhmī, Māheśvarī, Kaumārī, Vaiṣṇavī, Vārāhī, Indrāṇī, Cāmuṇḍā.
4. Seven Satīs–In Durgā Saptaśatī, there are three caritrās (a) Prathama (base); (b) Madhyama (middle); and (c) Uttama (apex). In each of these, there are several satis whose names are given below:

In the Prathama caritra, Mahākālī is the chief Śatī. The seven satīs of this caritra are: Kālī, Tārā, Chinnamastā, Sumukhī, Bhuvaneśvarī, Bālā and Kubjā. In the madhya caritra, Mahālakṣmī is the chief śatī. The seven satīs of this caritra are Lakṣmī, Lalitā, Kālī, Durgā, Gāyatrī, Arundhatī and Sarasvatī. In Uttama caritra, Mahāsarasvatī is the chief Śatī. The seven Śatīs of this caritra are Brāhmī, Māheśvarī, Kaumārī, Vaiṣṇavī, Vārāhī, Indrāṇī and Cāmuṇḍā.

This book further discusses the ten major incarnations of Viṣṇu. I have also given a description of Vedic deities. The major Vedic deities are Agni, Varuṇ, Yama, Indra, Sūrya and Vāyu. In the fourth section, textual and contextual significance of Vedic–Purāṇik and purely Purāṇik deities has been discussed. Gaṇeśa is the major deity of this category. Names of different deities have been explained according to their mythological background as well as scientifically in the present work. For example, Gaṇeśa is known by such name as Lambakarṇa (long-ear), Lambodara (long-belly), and Gajānana (elephant-headed). Foods of deities also have been similarly explained. Gaṇeśa likes Durvā (a grass), Laḍḍū (sweet ball) and Jambūphala. Kārtikeya (son of Śiva) has six heads. Hanumāna looks like a monkey. Śitalās vehicle is donkey. Meaning of all these symbols has been given in this book particularly for western readers. Westerners call Hanumāna the monkey-god, Gaṇeśa as the elephant-headed god. To dispel their ignorance about Indian deities is the major objective of the present work.

The book further provides a description of purely purāṇik and regional deities. Major deities of this category are Śitalā and Saṅkaṭhā. To collect matter on these deities, the author had to go through a large number of books available in Hindi and English languages.

Hindu literature is very vast. It consists of four Vedās, four sub-Vedās, Upaniṣads, eighteen Purāṇās, eighteen sub-Purāṇās, several law books, theology books, epics such as the Rāmāyaṇa and the Mahābhārata, several philosophical systems such as orthodox (six systems of philosophy) heterodox (Buddhist, Jain and Carvak philosophy), Buddha philosophy in Pālī and Sanskrit languages, Jain philosophy in Prākrit language. In addition to these, there is vast store of Tāntrik literature. Hindū literature is like an ocean. Even a single drop of this can bring real happiness to man.

Mine is the humble effort to present the kernel of the entire Hindū literature in my own way. Others more informed in this field are requested to take up the mission on a greater scale. In spite of my best efforts, certain errors might have crept into this work. Learned readers are requested to apprise me with such errors.

From the deep analysis of the accounts of gods and goddesses in the foregoing five sections, it appears that there pervades only one supreme substance in the universe which is variously named by the people. This Supreme Being is conceptualized according to one's own needs and requirement. Such a view of the universe is the very theme of the Vedic hymns and Purāṇās. In Ramtāpniyopaniṣad, it is said that the attributeless Brahma reincarnates itself in different forms for the good of the worshipper. An example, a Goldsmith makes several jewels from gold but in all the jewels the common substance is gold. Gram is another example. Gram is one and single substance. From this, countless eatables are prepared. The eatables are diverse in shape and taste but their primary content is one and the same i.e. gram.

The Supreme Being is one yet it has been conceptualised in the form of countless gods and goddesses. With these diversities are associated the methods and the processes of the worship of the respective deities. For example, in the Vedic mode of worship, particular emphasis is laid on fame, shape, and Sādhanā. In Soma, Aśvamedh and Purāṇik worship, stress is laid on prayer, recitation of name, pilgrimage, vows, fasting and so on. Similarly, for immediate outcome with lesser efforts and small cost, Tāntrik devices are applied. A few examples: A smaller secret formula (gaṁ gaṇapataye namaḥ) was evolved for Mṛtuñjaya mantra consisting of thirty-six letters. This has been done with a view to grab God's blessings with meagre efforts in lesser time. For such objectives, several mystic formulas are also applied. Traces of such mystic formulas are available in Upaniṣads, Vedic hymns and Purāṇas. But in Tantra Śāstra such formulas have been made more accessible and elaborate. For example, in Tantra literature such mysterious themes as presiding deity, shape, energy of *varṇamātrikā kavarg* are discussed in big details. Similarly, description, of sixty four Varṇās, their respective gods and goddesses, energy is available in Tantra Śāstra.

In Tantra literature Bījmātrās (kaṁ, khaṁ, and gaṁ) have been evolved. The first Bījamantra of Navārṇa is *aiṁ*. This Bījamantra has enormous power. *Aiṁ* consists of three letter a+e+a = *aiṁ*. The candrabindu in this mystic formula symbolises thrill-producing from E. The first mantra of Sāmveda starts from letter A. By joining these three letters aiṁ is formed. Later, the symbol of thrill-producing power in the form of candrabindu is added to it and thus *aiṁ* comes into being. So *aiṁ* symbolises the three Vedas. Tantra śāstra has evolved this Bījamantra by joining the three first letters of the three Vedas for the attainment of worldly objectives. Similarly, hrīṁ, klīṁ mystic formulas were also evolved.

Along with a power of varṇās, power of lines has also been brought out in the Tantra literature. For example, upward triangle symbolises the three powers of *māyā* of god namely, desire, knowledge and action. In God arises the desire to create. Then arises knowledge to create and finally the action follows. To symbolise this idea, the mystic formula of triangle has been cconceptualised.

The Triangle is of two kinds, *upward* and *downward*. The Downward triangle symbolises the creation aspect of the world. The Upward triangle symbolises Śiva, the supreme seat of Mokṣa and Bliss. The point between the two triangles symbolises energy. From this point arises movement which leads to creation.

Those interested in worldly attainment and possession should worship goddesses related to the downward triangle. Seekers of Mokṣa should opt for the upward triangle symbolising Śiva. Those seeking both *this worldly* and *other worldly* bliss must worship a six-angled diagram. Those seeking the worship omnipresent, omni permeating, supreme female energy (Parāmbika), must worship, śrīcakra. In śrīcakra, there are nine downward and nine upward triangles. This cakra symbolises the entire cosmos.

Similarly, there are Bhuvaneśvarī Yantra, Durgā Yantra, and Svastik Yantrās. The Svastik is the yantra of Gaṇeśa. Through this Yantra Gaṇeśa is worshipped and propitiated. He is regarded as the remover of all obstacles. In fact, it is very difficult to unravel the mysteries of all the Yantrās.

In Tantra Śāstra deities have been symbolised through letters and diagrams. Siddhis can be attained through the worship of numbers as well. Tantra Śāstra proclaims that through numbers charismatic siddhīs are attained. There are Yantrās with such numbers as fifteen, twenty and thirty. These number-Yantrās are progeny-generative, wealth-creative and health-creative.

Pt. Harendr Upadhyay

AUṀ

AUṀ

The concept of 'Aum/Om' is said to have been acknowl edged throughout the world beyond Alpha and Omega. It would be very interesting to dwell on the widespread and encyclopedic word 'Om', which is an eternal, mystical syllable. It is the syllable that signifies for the Universe. In order to have conspicuously and transparently clear concept of 'Om', its analytical interpretation is quite indispensable though it is beyond delineation and description. It consists of tri-syllables representing the blended intonations permeating through each and every particle of the Universe. Phonetically 'aum' can be analyzed thus:

'A' is produced in the throat so it is guttural. 'U' is considered to be middle, 'M' is pronounced with the lips and the nose so it is called the labial, and the nasal. If we profoundly ponder over this word, it is located at the centre of everything whether it may be an animate or inanimate object, a manifest or veiled thing. It having the divine and mystical power represents the mystery of the Ultimate Reality. Its pronunciation is made with a nasalized ending half way between 'M' is made with a nasalized ending half way between 'M' and 'N'. Really speaking, this is a primal sound. It is the word wherein there is the greatest amount of possibility of encompassment of the trinity of time, so to speak, the present, the past and the future. Again 'Auṁ' projects Time and the universe out of its nucleus just as a projector projects a series of pictures by means of the rays of light on to a screen. But there is a cardinal difference between the 'aum' as there exists nothing beyond the latter whereas there are countless things on the reverse side of the former. One is abstract: the other is concrete. One is destructible: the other is indestructible. 'Aum' stands for the Absolute who is known as Brahmā, Viṣṇu and Śiva having their respective salient features—creation, preservation and destruction. On the contrary, it marks the Universe composed of the triple manifestations of nature—sattvaguṇa (tranquility), Rajasguṇa (passionate activity) and tamasguṇa (inactivity inertia). From the esoteric standpoint it represents causal, carnal and astral bodies beyond which the soul and the Absolute are identical.

It is termed as a 'Bīj Mantra'. Just as in our practical life, we realise the importance preponderance of a seed, in the likewise manner a considerable degree of importance is attached to this Mantra. We derive an important string of information from the Vedas and the Upaniṣads that 'Bīja Mantra' is normally placed in front of all the other Mantras.

It is only 'Auṁ' that is, and that was, and that will be the subject of all the sciences, the different branches of knowledge.

It may satisfy the curiosity of the questioning minds of numerous disciples and pupils. It produces the desired result and has ability to hold everything like the vast ocean. It inspires all the monks, sages and seers. It refers to the transcendental world that is real. Life aims at 'Om' because it is the trinity of Reality, the one Truth, the one Good and the one Beauty (Satyam, Śivam and Sundaram) which are offered prayers in multi-fashions. Man is relieved of grief and pain by means of 'Om'. It is being and becoming both. It brings light, delight and peace all around. It can be said that 'Om' is the telephonic number of God for the sake of communication. It is chanted at the beginning of meditation, at the beginning and at the end of adoration and prayer. Even when Yoga is practiced, it is pronounced. The following poetic lines describe the presence of 'aum' in various forms and shades:

Body in extreme heat
Soft heart in beat
All find home
At last in Om
It gives light
Makes us bright
Endows divine sight
Its very clear expression
Produces lasting impression
If every thing is fruit
Om in the real sense root

VEDIC DEITIES

GAṆEŚA

Gaṇeśa is such a deity as is beyond Prakṛti and Puruṣ. The analytical and metaphorical meaning of the word 'Gaṇeśa' runs thus:

Gaṇeśa = Ga + ṇ + ī + ś
Ga–Stands for the physical world.
ṇ–Signifies the spiritual world.

In this way, Gaṇeśa stands for the deity who commands and masters both the physical and the spiritual worlds.

Gaṇeśa is called 'Acyut' as he never deviates from the right path. 'A' of Acyut' stands for 'not' and Cyuta implies to deviate'. He is also known as Vighneśawara (remover of hurdles). He is the master of celibates. Swastika Cinha (a mark of fylfot) is the appearance of Gaṇapati.

Gaṇapati = Gaṇ + Pati

Ṇ denotes a group of five senses and of five action organs, a host of men, a galaxy of deities and a group of demons. 'Pati' stands for a master or a chief i.e. one who is the master and the controller of organs, men, deities and demons. 'Gaṇ' stands for Sat, Citta and Ānanda. It represents earth, heaven and space and shows the three states of mind-conscious, sub-conscious and unconscious. From the physical point of view, Gaṇeśa is the son of Śiva and Pārvatī: on the contrary, from the spiritual point of view, he is not anyone's son as he himself created lots of deities like Brahmā, Śiva etc. for the good of mankind, just as many incarnations like Rāma, Kṛṣṇa, Vārāha, Kacchapa, Matsya etc., refer to Viṣṇu. That is why he is worshipped not only among five deities but also among thirty three crore deities. He is also regarded as a Vedic deity. He incarnated himself at the outset of the creation for the welfare of his devotees.

According to Gaṇeśa Purāṇa, he incarnated himself in various forms. In Kṛta Yuga (the Golden Age) he was reputed to be Mahotakata Vināyaka having ten arms. He was seated on a lion. In Dvāpar Yuga (the Silver Age), he was famous as Mayureśwara who sat on a peacock. He was lustrous in his appearance and had six arms. In Tretā Yuga (the copper Age), he earned popularity as Gajānan or Gaurīputra mounting on a rat. He was of saffron colour. In Kali Yuga (the Iron Age), he earned name and fame as Dhumraketu possessing two arms. His appearance is of smoky complexion.

On the basis of Mudgal Purāṇa, Gaṇeśa principally incarnated himself eight times (having different forms):

> 1. Vakratuṇḍa; 2. Ekadanta; 3. Mahodar; 4. Gajānan; 5. Lambodar; 6. Vikata; 7. Vighnarāja; and 8. Dhumravarṇa. Besides, he is also called by different names: Sumukha, Kapila, Gajakarṇa, Vighnāsan, Vināyaka, Dhumraketu, Gaṇādhyakṣa, and Bhālacandra.

Gaṇeśa has an elephant's head. He possesses a pot-belly. He is yellow or red complexioned. Siddhi (accomplishment or miraculous power) and Buddhi (discretion) are considered to be Gaṇeśa's consorts. At the same time, Lābha and Kṣema are said to be his sons.

He is of short stature which points out that a social worker should possess the qualities like meekness and simplicity in order that not any sense of pride may occur to him. The major portion of his body corresponds to the human body but he has an elephant's head that shows the principal centre of thinking power. The elephant itself stands predominantly for discretion, patience and seriousness. His ears symbolise patience and solemnity; his pot-belly stands for the capacity for keeping good and bad things inside itself but when they are needed, they should be at once given expression; Ekadant is the symbol of unity and solidarity. Laḍḍū (sweets-ball) stands for a well organised society; Cinnabar (Sulphuric Oxide) which graces the radiant appearance of Gaṇeśa, signifies good fortune.

Certain blades of grass that are offered to him, stand for meekness, delight and good luck. A rat is the vehicle of Gaṇeśa. It has two contradictory qualities. On the one hand, it is regarded as a creature of bad tendencies. On the other hand, it is said to be next to the immanent god who brings the noble qualities and good things to light by eliminating bad things and evil qualities from the world.

He possesses four arms which point to the four important directions—the first defends the deities dwelling inside the heaven, the second mankind, the third demons and the fourth Nāgas. The three arms are armed with the three types of important and valuable items, such as, a book, a goad, and a sweet-ball. A book stands for the removal of illusion. A goad is a device for control. A tooth is the symbol of Brahma (the Supreme Being). The large ears of Gaṇeśa represent a device which minutely discriminates between merits and demerits, illusion and the Ultimate Reality.

BRAHMĀ

Brahmā is the name of consciousness or the supreme creative spirit that appeared from the fathomless ocean of the super-consciousness or Supreme Being. He is the creator of the creation of animate and inanimate objects. According to the Ṛg Veda, the most ancient scripture, the term 'Brahmā' was put to use to denote the mysterious power that was implied in the hymns or sacred utterances. Afterwards they came to be pronounced by a host of holy men. The very men were referred to as Brahmins. According to the Purāṇas, Brahmā appeared from a lotus-flower that had already sprung from the navel of Lord Viṣṇu.

Though Brāhma is regarded as the grand-father of all the deities, demons and creatures, yet he always favours and advocates religion in a particular way.

He also becomes the instrumental cause of the twenty four incarnations of Viṣṇu. By means of Prajāpati, he continues to create the subjects in the world, so he is called the master of Prajāpati. He was blessed with the ten sons who were born according to Purāṇs by wish, not by coition. The names of the sons are given below:

1. Mārici; 2. Atṛ; 3. Angirā 4. Pulastya; 5. Pulah; 6. Ṛtu; 7. Prachetā; 8. Vaśiṣṭha; 9. Bhṛgu; and 10. Nārada.

It is significant to mention that Brahmā, Viṣṇu and Maheśa incarnated themselves out of the combination of the culmination of the three qualities of Prakṛti (Nature).

Brahmā possesses the four faces but virtually only the three are seen. The matted and braided hair graces his head. He has large beard. He is always bound engrossed in profound meditation. He is four handed. In one hand, he holds a water jug (a ritual artefact) containing water which symbolises life. He carries a particular volume of water just as a mother possesses a child in her womb, in the same way, she is endowed with milk in her breast in order that she many nourish and nurture it. His four arms stand for the four stages of life, such as, childhood, teenage, adulthood and old-age. The four heads stand for the four directions, four eras. The four crowns stand for the four types of responsibility as well as reverence. His beard does not denote physical age but the maturity and profundity of knowledge. For this, he is credited with the suitable and sublime title of a grand-father. His moustache signifies honour and self-respect. The garland stands for different types of creations. One of his hands shows a blessing pose. The other holds a scripture which symbolises knowledge and learning. A swan is his vehicle that represents the individual soul. It is of white complexion which is the symbol of truth, righteousness and satoguṇa (one of the three attributes of nature). Just as it differs between milk and water, in the same way, the soul in appearance of a swan discriminates between the noble and the ignoble, the good and the evil, the right and the wrong. It also stands for non-attachment and renunciation.

VIṢṆU

Viṣṇu is the name of the ineffable, resplendent, transcendental and the Ultimate Reality. He is the beginning and endless that is to say, he is not subject to birth and death. He is the primal cause of the creation. He is omnipresent, omniscient and omnipotent. Each thing emanates from him. He is not perceived through the sense organs and physical actions and is not confined to any name. As God, he lives in everyone's mind. He is the master of yajñasa (a holy sacrifice).

The word 'Viṣṇu' is derived from the root word 'Viṣ' which means 'to enter'. In other words, he runs through or pervades the whole universe to maintain it, this is why he is called 'Viṣṇu'. Though he is one, he takes on various forms for the good and welfare of man-kind. From the gigantically single divine embodied spirit of Viṣṇu, thirty three crore deities like Brahmā, Indra, Rudra, Varuṇa (Neptune), Kubera (Mammon), Agni (Fire), Vāyu (Air), Sūrya (Sun), and Dikpāla etc., were born. He incarnated himself twenty four times. Here the names of those twenty-four incarnations are being given below:

1. Sankādi; 2. Varāha (a boar); 3. DevarṣI; 4. Nārāyaṇa; 5. Kapilmuni; 6. Dattātreya; 7. Yajña; 8. Ṛṣabha; 9. Ādirāg Pṛthu; 10. Matsya (fish); 11. Kūrma (a turtle);

12. Danwantri; 13. Mohini; 14. Nṛsiṁha (man-lion); 15. Vāman (a dwarf); 16. Hayagrīva; 17. Harī; 18. Paraśurāma (one who always holds a battle-axe); 19. Vyāsa; 20. Haṇsa (a swan); 21. Rāma; 22. Kṛṣṇa; 23. Buddha; and 24. Kalki.

Viṣṇu reclines in the soft-bed of the coils of the multi-headed serpent-king; śeṣanāga. Lakṣmī is his consort. Brahmā, the creator of the universe and one of the three triads of Hindu mythology, emanates from the hollow tubular stalk of a lotus which has sprung from the navel of Viṣṇu who is of blue complexion. His head is graced with a jewelled crown. He has numerous arms but practically, only four are perçeptible.

His first hand contains a wheel, the second a conch shell, the third a mace and the fourth a lotus-flower. In all his arms, he wears bracelets which are gem studded. He mounts an eagle (Garuḍa). This is a half-man and a half-bird as a vehicle. Sometimes he is shown sitting on a lotus. Many sorts of rings become his fingers. He is dressed in yellow. The conch shell represents water, removal of pride, purity, honesty, righteousness, salvation, satoguṇa (one of the three attributes of nature representing purity and goodness) and the origin of existence. The wheel stands for the Universal Mind and energies of the creation and annihilation. The mace symbolises the power of knowledge and enlightenment. The four arms stand for the four forms such as, anḍaja (Something that is formed from an egg).

Piṇḍaja (an animal which is born from embryo), Uṣmaja or Ukhamaja (insects and worms that are born in the summer season), and Sthāwara (immovable property) four states of life—conscious (wakefulness), sub-conscious, unconscious and blessedness. It is the human creation which is shaped by Brahmā's four sons who were born not by coition but by mind according to Hindu mythology—Sanaka, Sanandan,

Sanatkumara and Sanātan, four Āśramas (the four religious orders referable to the different periods of a Brahman's life), Brahmacarya (Student), Garhasthya (house-holder), Vānaprastha (anchorite) and Sannyās (recluse).

The two ear-rings stand for the mortal body and the individual soul. Sometimes he has eight arms holding a conch shell, a wheel, a club, a bow, an arrow, a battle-axe, a lasso and a cleaver. They (eight arms) stand for Dharma (religion) Jnāna (knowledge), Virāga (non-attachment), Aiśvarya (majesty or glory), Adharma (unrighteousness or irreligion), Agyāna (ignorance), Avirāga (Non-attachment) and Anaiśvarya (absence of majesty). The club stands for knowledge and discrction. Thc lotus-flower signifies earth, world and also six Aiśvaryas (majesty): Jñāna (knowledge), Lakṣmī (riches), Vairāgya (non-attachment), Dharma (religion) and Yaśa (fame), a Yajñopavīta (a sacred thread stands for AUM), Praṇava. The yellow cloth symbolises the Vedas. The bracelets and the garlands stand for the constellation of stars. The eagle (Garuḍa) stands for the three Vedas. Its two wings represent knowledge and action.

The four weapons are the symbol of the objects of man's creation and existence (Puruṣārtha): Dharma (religion), Artha (Wealth), Kama (sex), Mokṣa (salvation).

SŪRYA

The great sun God (the God of Light) apparently and visibly occupies a valuable and estimable position in the midst of the various Vedic deities. He abounds with a stream of abundant light and lustre viz. the source of light. He is fraught with life, vitality, fame, eyes, ear, souls and minds. He enlightens and illumines the entire world. He is reputed to be the creator of the wheel of time. He is of golden complexion in his appearance. He is also compared to a China rose. He wears a dress dyed in red like vermilion. His neck is garlanded and some other parts of his body are embellished with ornaments. He is seated on a blood coloured lotus. He is four handed. The three hands hold a lotus-flower, a conch-shell and a wheel and the fourth is expressive of a defensive pose. But occasionally, the two hands carry the lotus-flowers and the next two represent fearless and blessing poses. Aruṇa (aura) is his charioteer. The chariot has seven horses or a seven headed-horse.

He is regarded as the lord of all planets. He blesses every one with wealth, glory and joy. The existence of days and nights are due to the sun. During the six months from the month of Māgha when the sun is on the north of the equator, the motion of his is fast in the night and slow in the day.

He is the manifestation par excellence of Viṣṇu and the guardian deity of the eyes. His incarnation is known as Mārtaṇḍa.

According to Brahmasūtra, Āditya is considered to be the Ultimate Reality. The Vedas also say that he is the creator, observer and destroyer.

Just as Viṣṇu, the observer, abides in Vaikuṇṭha (the abode of gods-paradise), Śiva on the magnificent crest of a mountain, named Kailāś, Brahmā, the creator, in Brahmloka, (in the eternal residence of the god Brahmā) in the same way, the sun in Ādityaloka (the abode of the sun or the solar system).

He is the eye of the whole world. The universe is created out of the sun at the outset and gets dissolved herein at last. The wheel stands for the Universal Mind and energies of creation and annihilation of the cosmos. The four arms symbolise simultaneously Aṇḍaja (born from an egg, as a bird, fish, snake), Piṇḍaja (an animal which is born from embryo viviparous, Uṣmajā (insects and worms that are born in the summer) and sthāvara (immovable property trees) the four states of life conscious (wakefulness), sub-conscious, unconscious and blessedness. The conch-shell represents the removal of pride, purity, honesty, righteousness, salvation, sattvaguṇa. The seven rays represent the seven horses or seven metres.

AGNIDEVA

In the very opening of this chapter, it would be fascinatingly interesting to give free expression to the fact that this creation is the handiwork of the Supreme Being and it is composed of the five elementary elements—earth, water, air, fire and ether—which, later on were personified as the five deities possessing different salient features. The God of fire Vulcan is one of them. He is in prominence when he plays cardinal part in Yajña, the religious sacrifice, which is not only for the attainment of worldly or heavenly happiness but also for the realization of God. He runs through each and every particle of the universe. Various types of gems come out of Fire. He is *Indra*, the Sun, *Rudra* and the Vital Air (Oxygen). He is the main deity among all the gods either in heaven or on earth.

Ṛg, the most ancient scripture in the midst of the Vedas refers to *Agni* at the outset. Again *Agni* is the first invention in the literature of the world as far as a word is concerned. He holds the second position among the gods after *Indra*. He is the guardian deity of the South-East quarter. He is portrayed as a crimson coloured personality with two to seven arms, and three legs. His black-red eyes, eyebrows and hair look bewitching. He assumes various forms. Operatively, he functions inside the body of an animal as the fire of the stomach which helps to digest food. He pervades the submarine, the forest-conflagration, the solar system, the manifested and the incomprehensible objects as well as the lightning in the midst of the several patches of clouds across the welkin. He manifests himself as the flames of the funeral pyre and takes the corpse as an offering.

Motion, effulgence, heat, digestion, and so forth are the diverse functions of the same energy. Modern science has also substantiated and proved it on the ground of a series of experiments. The god of Fire is the presiding deity of this energy. He is the priest of gods. He works as the liaison between gods and men. *Dharma*, religion, is his father, *Vasubhāryā* is his mother. *Swādhā*, a word used when making an offering to manes, and *Swāhā*, a word uttered while making an offering to a dcity, are his consorts. His vehicles are a ram and a goat. He is beautifully garlanded with fruit. He holds mainly a spoon, a fan, a cup, a spear in his hands. He is two headed. His tummy has bulged out.

His two heads symbolise earth and heaven, the phenomenal and noumenal standpoints. His beard stands for non-attachment and a moustache for valour and prestige. His seven arms represent seven days-Sunday, Monday, Tuesday, Wednesday, Thursday, Friday and Saturday; Seven elements of the human body intra cellular fluid–blood, muscles, fat, bone, marrow and semen seven kinds of joys; the seven notes in music; the continents of the whole word; the ceremony of going round the fire seven times on the auspicious occasion of marriage; the seven underworlds, viz. '*Atala*', '*Vitala*', '*Sutala*', '*Rasātala*', '*Talātal*', '*Mahātala*' *and* '*Pātāla*; the seven principal places of pilgrimage '*Ayodhyā*', '*Mathurā*', '*Kāśī*', '*Kāñcī*', '*Ujjain*', *and* '*Dvārikā*'; a group of seven principal sages, a group of seven stars called the Great Bear. The garland signifies the result of actions and the state of being endowed with goodness. The vehicles are the symbol of energy.

VARUṆA

Varuṇa is the name of the deity who represents water. It is for this reason that there is a graceful and fine portrayal of him and that he is regarded as the god of all the fathomless oceans in most of our mythological books. According to Greek Mythology, the same position is held by Neptune. He is of white complexion because the appearance of water is effulgently white i.e. spotlessly clean. A giant fish is treated as his vehicle. There lies much likeness between him and a white conch or crystal. His neck is ornamented nicely with a white wreath. His hand is armed with a lasso. He wears an armlet and a crown. He possesses the head as well as the twine legs of an antelope. But sometimes he is two handed and sometimes he is four handed. His vehicle is also found with four legs (the four fins).

The one head stands for only one objective to wit, to bless every sort of creature with life. Remarkably, water is life. The one leg stands for life and existence and the other for death. The four hands symbolise the four ages:

Satyayuga (the first, the golden age)
Dvāparayuga (the second, the silver age)
Tretāyuga (the third, copper age)
Kaliyuga (the fourth iron age)

During these four ages, he supplies water to every creature without discrimination. The four fins or legs of his vehicle are the symbol of Prithvīloka (the mortal world) Devaloka (the world of deities), Yamaloka (the world of death), Pitṛloka (the world of manes) He travels through the four worlds with the help of his vehicle.

To sum up, this deity is not subject to any country, caste or creed but he figures throughout the world.

VĀYU

Scientifically, the wind is a mixture of different types of gases that surround the earth. One of them is the vital air which we breathe. Normally it does not have any hue or colour.

On the other hand, according to religious scriptures, there is the personification and glorification of the wind, i.e. Vāyu is treated as a deity whose complexion is stated to be green whereas in accordance with Matsya Purāṇa, he is smoky coloured. From the Yogic point of view, the deer being the vehicle of the wind conveys a special significance. Vāyu is also reputed to be Cakra Anahada (the heart's centre from where divine melody is produced).

He looks very handsome. He wanders, up and down in his chariot that is fraught with dazzling light. It is drawn by a pair of horses. Sometimes, there is phenomenal increase in the number of his horses i.e. forty-nine or one thousand. Sometimes, he is two handed and sometimes four. His two hands are fitted with a book and a wheel. The next two refer to a protective pose and something mystical. At times, the first one is armed with a thunder–bolt (Vajra) which is the symbolic representation of the destruction of all kinds of ignorance as well as the quality of invincibility or invulnerability. The second is fitted with a flag which is the symbol of victory and triangular power.

The wind is known as the vital air. His face is expressive of peace and tranquillity. He is seen raising his eye-brows.

There are five kinds of prāṇas or vital air in our body: Vyāna (excretory), Apāna (evacuatory), Samāna (that which creates disturbance), Prāṇa (respiration) and Udāna (transforming energy). One of them holds the most important position for the sustenance of life.

According to the most ancient scriptures, Vāyu is regarded as Brahmā. He is omnipresent and mobile. There is throbbing and pulsation because of him. The mind, matter, vital air and intellectual power are at the disposal of him. All the creatures derive energy from the air that is activated by the sun, the source of inspiration to gods. The air purges and purifies the whole world. He is known by different names.

INDRA

It is Indra who predominates and carries great value and im portance in the Vedic age. He is reputed to be the deity of rain and thunder. He reigns in the kingdom wherein all the gods reside. He is golden complexioned and is four handed. He possesses a conch-shell, a net, a bow, a goad, an arrow and a thunder-bolt in his respective hands. He has one thousand eyes in all his body. Airāvata, the king of white elephants, is the vehicle of Indra.

According to the Upaniṣads, Indra is one whose means are the organs which represent a goddess in the body. In other words, 'Indriyas' (organs of the body) are closely connected with Indra as the former derive energy from the latter.

He has unlimited power. When the sun is under the influence of one of the nine principal planets, the mythological dragon' head is supposed to devour the sun or moon during an eclipse. Indra vanquishes this demon and supplies light to the sun. In the absence of the sun and the moon, representing the two divine and powerful torches of the universe as well as day and night, he himself fills the world with light and luster. It is only he that has been worshipped by different names like the sun and Viṣṇu etc. Thirty five names are recorded in Amara Koṣa. He has three wives, whose names are Pulomana, Śaci and Indrāṇī. The place where he dwells is popularly known as Amarawati. His charioteer's name is Motāli. His garden is

known as Nandan and the name of his palatial building is Vaijanātha and his son's name is Jayanta.

Indra stands for the soul and Airāwata for truth, honesty dutifulness, earnestness, endurance and violence.

At the commencement of each manvantara (tenure of Manu, the progenitor of the human race i.e., the fourteenth part day of Brahmā) the post of the Lord of paradise continues to change. One, who performs one hundred horse-sacrifices, becomes Indra as a universal monarch in a Manvantara. At present, the seventh Manvantara is going on. In the Vedic age, he held the most important position among all the gods. He protected gods, priest, cows and cow herds. But during the age of the Purāṇas, he began losing his value and importance. In this way, human shortcomings started developing in him. His idols are rarely found in temples yet he has been extolled to the skies at numerous places in the Vedas and many other scriptures.

THE INCARNATIONS OF VISNU

MATSYA (FISH)

Matsya is one of the twenty four incarnations of Viṣṇu, the Ultimate Reality. He possesses the lower part of his body like that of a fish as well as the upper part like that of a man. Being golden complexioned, he is radiant and lustrous in appearance. His body measures about million miles in length. His head is crowned with the horn. He is four handed. In all of them, he holds a mace, a conch shell, a lotus-flower and a wheel. Sometimes, his two hands are seen in the defensive and blessing poses. In order to show mercy on the creatures and to defend the Vedas, he clothed his spirit with a body himself as a fish.

This excellent incarnation has been propounded by some important scriptures like the Bhagavada Purāṇa, Mahābhārata and Matsya Purāṇa. By this incarnation, he saved the life of the primal progenitor of mankind. He also restored the Vedas to Brahmā from whom Hayagrīva, the great demon had stealthily taken away.

KŪRMA (TORTOISE)

The tortoise, an incarnation of Viṣṇu, holds one of the most important positions amidst his all other incarnations. The worshipful adoration of the Almighty Supreme Being in this form bears a testimony to omnipresence. In the initial phase of the creation, for the first time, a tortoise, a fish and a boar etc. came into being. The tortoise represents the vital air.

This incarnation is also known as Kūrma which refers to a cycle of Brahmā (a mere day of the creator Brahmā is equal to 4,320,000,000 human years). He is in the form of a half-man as well as a half turtle, he is four armed and in the upper and the lower, he holds a wheel, a conch shell, a mace and a lotus-flower but occasionally, his two hands symbolise the poses of protection and blessing. His back measures one lac yojana (A yojana is a measure of distance roughly thirteen kilometres) in length on which the high mountain Maura is located.

The conch shell stands for the glory of saintly figures. The interior hereof signifies the infinite space which expands in a clockwise rotation. If its motion is anti-clockwise, the laws of nature are reversed. The lotus-flower stands for mystical power, joy, beauty purity and non-attachment.

The wheel is the symbol of completion and enlightenment. The mace stands for the power of natural laws and time which roots out darkness of ignorance.

VĀRĀHA

Vārāha, the Boar, is one of the significant incarnations of Viṣṇu. His head is like that of a boar and the remaining body resembles the human one. He has four arms. But sometimes he is seen with the two arms. All of his hands are equipped with a wheel, a conch shell, a mace and a lotus-flower. But with the two arms, he assumes a slightly different pose, that is to say, the one is furnished with a mace, and the other is expressive of a blessing pose.

According to the Purāṇas (the mythological books), somewhere he is related with Vāyu (Air) and somewhere with the founder of a religious sacrifice (yajña).

Remarkably, the earth exists on the jaw or jowl of the Boar as it (the earth) was covered with snow through and through. But after a while, it was cleared of snow by the hot rays of the sun. The force which was functioning is still functioning and will function even in the mirror of futurity.

In accordance with Vajrayāna Buddhism related in the Tantra Granth, Varāha stands for a Divine Boar cycle (Kalpa = a Brahmā's day) conditioned by the time. 'Var' means super i.e. the soul. One, who envelops it, is regarded as Varāha. It is Kāla Sattā (the existence of death) that envelops it. This is the reason that Kāla Śakti (the force of death) is named Varāhi.

In order to rescue the earth, Viṣṇu as Varāha came down to the bottom of the ocean. As it is evident that the earth had already been abducted by a great demon who was put to death by Varāha.

NARSIṀHA

Narasiṁha is the fourth incarnation of Lord Viṣṇu. He takes the form of a half-man as well as half-lion. He is four handed. He holds a conch-shell and a wheel in two hands and the next two are expressive of benedictory and protective poses. His yellowish eyes are just like beaten out gold. His face is astonishingly glowing due to the golden hair of his neck and face. His jowls are enormous. Having his bitter and sharp tongue like a knife, crooked eye-brows, cocked ears, bulging nose, wide-open mouth like the cave of a mountain, bifurcated jaws, broad chest, slender waist and hundreds of arms spreading to the four winds, he assumes an awfully hideous appearance.

In order to slay Hiraṇyakaśyapa, the demon-king, and to defend Prahlāda, the great devotee, Viṣṇu incarnated himself. It marks the triumph of non-violence over violence. Prahlād, the worshipper of truth, stands for Satoguṇa (First of the three qualities according to the Hindu Philosophy of the life representing righteousness, purity, truth and goodness) and Hiraṇyakaśyapa for violence and Tamoguṇa (last of the three qualities of nature, the one pertaining to gloominess or ignorance). At the outset, a small and graceful size and guise but in the end of the dwarf immeasurably rises.

VĀMANA (DWARF)

The incarnation of Vāmana holds a prominent and singular place and position amidst the twenty four incarnations of Viṣṇu, who in the Vedic literature, from the spiritual point of view, is the most gigantic and powerful deity. He, in the graceful garb of a dwarf, stands on the ten toes of his feet. He has a vase in one hand as well as an umbrella in the other. A ring made of Kuś (a kind of grass) suits his middle finger. Sometimes he is seen with a scripture in one of hands. An ear-ornament is dangling. His hair is long and some portion of his body is wrapped in a deer-skin. He appears in a human form whereas his previous ones are quite different.

Remarkably, he has three legs which symbolise speech, mind and vital air. A dwarf stands for the underdeveloped stage of mankind.

Disguising himself as a dwarf, Viṣṇu exercised his astonishingly supernatural power to pervade heaven and earth, nether-world merely in two steps as well as to protect and provide deliverance to all the creatures through Bali "who was the demon-king and but he never failed to culminate in name and fame" the grand son of Prahlāda.

PARAŚURĀMA

Paraśurāma, the youngest son of Jamadāgni, who extirpated the Kśatriyas from the transitory world twenty one times, is the marvellous rage-incarnation of Vīṣṇu who manifests himself for the first time in human form. He is credited with the suitable epithet of Paraśurāma in virtue of having a paraśu (a battleaxe) with him. He has a fair complexioned personality with the scattered matted and braided hair on his head. He wears the skin of an antelope (dear skin) together with and armour inlaid with the two divine lights–the sun and the moon.

He is the great warrior, a hermit. He has the greatest amount of love for the learning of weapons. He is generally shown as having two arms which carry a battleaxe as well as a bow but ever and anon appears with the four ones bearing an arrow, a bow, a battle-axe, a sword. The battle-axe symbolises something that conquers darkness and ignorance and also brings man to the spiritual path from worldly ties. The arrow stands for male energy and also the power of love and the bow, the five human senses and awareness. The sword represents wisdom and enlightenment.

RĀMA

Rāma is the unparalleled and matchless symbol of the cultural achievement of India. Through his cosmic play, he has been the central and cardinal source of divine inspiration to mankind playing the role of an eminent person whose life has been elegantly depicted in literary works. He is shown as a great and benevolent hero on the vast stage of the world. When gripped in political topsy-turvy, social upheaval and cultural crises, we remember him to seek a very valuable lesson from his qualities like patience, dutifulness, bravery, endurance, steadfastness, fidelity, large-heartedness and so forth.

The Etymological meaning of 'Rāma' is: One who pervades the inner core of those personalities who are blessed with the yogic power as well as animate and inanimate objects, is considered to be Rāma. Being the eternal pillar of religion, he is regarded as the seventh incarnation of Viṣṇu. He is, undoubtedly, God. In the previous times, at the request of Brahmā, the creator of the world, he incarnated himself to kill Rāvaṇa, the demon-king of Lankā. Practically, he was born with a silver spoon in a royal family. Daśaratha, the king of Ayodhyā, was credited with being the father of Rāma. In the same way, Yogamāyā also incarnated herself as Sītā. Later on, she became his consort. He is also called Maryadā Puruṣottam whose life was, from every standpoint, graced with bright ideal. He is subject-loving. Not only in normal but also in abnormal circumstances, he attached great value and importance to religion and ideal. It can be illustrated by an example: on the battlefield, whenever a ten-headed demon was deprived of arms and weapons, the valiant Rāma did not fight with him.

We derive a historical description of Rāma from the Ṛgveda, the Purāṇas, the Mahābhārata, the Rāmāyaṇa, Buddhist Jātakas and many other important works of Indian literature. There is much written about the kings belonging to the solar race. But it is astoundingly baffling that there is less description of Rāma. According to the Mahābhārata and the Rāmāyaṇa, the greatest amount of importance is given to the mention of his ideal personality. In accordance with the genecology in the Purāṇas, he ruled over Ayodhyā in the sixty first generation of the Ikṣhvaku dynasty but in order to carry out his father's orders, he renounced his kingdom and proceeded to the forest.

The cosmic play or sport by him is confined not only to India, but also to a number of foreign countries like China, Ceylon (Lanka), Indonesia, Iran, Mongolia, Tibet, Africa, Mauritius and so forth. Much information has been collected from a series of excavations at various important places. They serve us a good deal of information pertaining to him.

He possesses two arms. In one hand, he holds a bow with arrows. The bow symbolises Prakṛti (a female figure) and arrows stand for a male figure. At last I would like to say that the pronunciation of the word 'Rāma' provides mental peace and physical health. Scientifically, when we pronounce 'Rā', our mouth opens wide, and consequently, the inside air comes out and pure air enters but when we pronounce 'Ma' the mouth is closed.

LORD KṚṢṆA

There are numerous incarnations of the Supreme, Pure consciousness (Parabrahman). Lord Kṛṣṇa is one of them. Though, in this regard, it is worth mentioning that he is not the incarnation but God Himself. The Purāṇas, the Śṛmadbhagad and the Upaniṣads bear the testimony to this fact. He is considered to be the eighth incarnation of Viṣṇu. In the midst of all the ten incarnations, he hold an estimable and important position. He is absolute eternal and the ocean of all the good and noble qualities like enlightenment, knowledge, glory, majesty, mercy and beauty.

According to Bhagavad–Gītā, Kṛṣṇa is said to be the omnipotent and Universal Soul having thousands of heads, thousands of eyes and thousands of legs. The sky is his head; the air is his vital one and so forth.

It is ordained by the scriptures that there is the threefold light of the Supreme Being. Accordingly, this very threefold light he manifested himself in the world to perform the cosmic play. In Kurukṣetra, he is graced with profound knowledge, energy, perfection and truth. In Dvārakā as well as Mathurā, he is fraught with the higher consciousness and greater power of activity. In Vṛṇdāvana, he is endowed with the highest degree of delight and desirability.

Generally he continued to perform his perpetual cosmic play in the creation which is indispensable to inculcate in the

human mind a sublime and noble notion with regard to duty and responsibility. In other words, the infinite playing is the finite. At present it is beyond me and even in future will be beyond me out and out, as he is endless and his play is correspondingly considered endless. It would be interesting to know that the cosmic play in Vraja is said to be that of sacred love. This incarnate, extraordinary, exceptional and matchless theatrical performance of the religious sacrifice of love was not only confined to amusement but also to the good of the world. By means of this play, he presented the real, pure and consistent ideal of love to the public. He was a stage manager of this drama. All the characters were attracted towards him. No one was selfish but all of them had already consigned their worthless things of selfishness to the conflagration of love. But the true and perfect model of the purest and highest love of God is Gopikās. In this way, this type of love is a very conspicuous example in the history of the world.

The incarnations of Rāma and Kṛṣṇa are well known throughout the world. The former is reputed to be maryādāpuruṣottam (as far as honour is concerned, he is the best among men) and the latter is entitled Līlāpuruṣotama (he is regarded as the best among men as far as his cosmic play is concerned). One is serious and the other's face wears a smile and hilarious expression. Vice versa, some western thinkers also speak their mind with regard to Kṛṣṇa. He, the Indian Hercules, excelled all men in the strength of body and spirit. He had purged the whole earth and sea of evil and founded many cities, and after his death, divine honours were paid. The Indian Hercules is especially worshipped by the Sourasenians, an Indian nation in whose land are two great cities Mathura and Cleisobar and through it flows a navigable river Johares (Jumna).

The Indian Hercules, according to Cicero, was called Belus. He is then the same as Bala, the brother of Kṛṣṇa and both are conjointly worshipped at Muttra; indeed they are considered to be one avatāra or incarnation of Viṣṇu. Bala is represented as a stout man with a club in his hand. He is called also Balarāma. As Bala, springing from Viṣṇu or Harī, he is certainly Hericula, Heri-Cullas, and Hercules.

The aim of the incarnation of Kṛṣṇa was to put the evil king Kansa to death. As it had already been prophesised that the eighth issue of Devakī would put him (Kansa) to death. This was the reason that he ordered his jailor to incarcerate Vasudeva, his brother in law, and sister (Devakī) too.

He is blue skinned, and has two hands. He is shown as blowing the flute extra ordinarily and bewitchingly. He is mainly dressed in yellow but in accordance with lots of changes in his cosmic plays, there is also a great change in his clothes. This is why he wears various types of colourful clothes. He is graced with ornaments. Sometimes one of his hands is armed with a conch-shell. He is seen in the midst of cows and cowherds. Rādhā is his consort. He also plays the role of Arjun's charioteer. The allegorical meaning of the word Kṛṣṇa-

Kṛ + ṣ + ṇa
Kṛ stands for truth
ṣ for consciousness
ṇ for bliss

The word conjointly symbolises cough, one of the humours of the body in the form of wind, bile, Sattva, Rajas and Tamas (equilibrium, passion and annihilation), action, speech and mind.

Again K + R + Ī
K stands for Kṛṣṇa bīj (seed)
R for God
Ī for Mahāmāyā (The great illusion)
Kṛṣṇa is synonymous with Auṁ
The mystical meaning–

Vāsudeva stands for Puruṣa;
Devakī for Prakṛti and Mathurā for the human body
Nandarājā for delight
Yaśoda for hope
Gopikās for the organs of the body
A group of gopās for the soul and meditation,
cow-herds for Kṛṣṇa's har
Vraja for the conscience of a man
Rādhā for Parāśakti
Kansa for arrogance
Vṛndāvan for triguṇatimakā
Rāslīlā for rāsabhairava
The flute for Anahad Anāda (word)
Love for a formula
Yamunā for meditation
Kṛṣṇa for the Ultimate Reality
The cow for earth

To sum up, Viṣṇu and Kṛṣṇa are not different i.e. both are the same. They are regarded as the sun. The sun's rays are considered to be Gopikās. Though these rays belong to the sun, they seem to be different and in the long run, they are merged in the sun. In the same way, Gopikas appear to be different from Kṛṣṇa, yet all of them are identical. In this way, they get mingled with Kṛṣṇa and the stage is known as the cosmic play of God.

From the dawn to dusk of life, he faced lots of hardship, calamity, suffering and corrupt practices. In spite of adverse circumstances, he never got disheartened. But he gave an inspiring and divine message to mankind to have patience and steadfastness by playing the role of a messenger of peace on the battle-field of Kurukṣetra.

BUDDHA

From both standpoints religious and historical, we envisage Lord Buddha. The former points out that he is the incarnation of Viṣṇu. He always appears to be engrossed in profound meditation. His palms and feet possess the lovely impression of a lotus-flower. He is enthroned on a lotus-flower and is clothed in yellow. He has two hands which represent blessing as well as protective postures.

It is fit for being written that this incarnation is quite different from all other incarnations. As Buddha, Viṣṇu shabbily dressed or in a dirty garb gave a string of advice to a host of demons to go against the authenticity of the Vedas and yajña. They (the demons) caused violence leading sin to as a result of which they were robbed of their power and preponderance. Taking advantage of their weakness, gods setup their sovereignty regained paradise but in this regard it is not less indispensable to know previously how demons and giants preponderated over gods in their influence and power by following the path suggested by Lord Indra i.e. he preached them to perform yajña and act according to the Vedas. They also started bearing hard on and excruciate gods to dispossess them of their paradise.

Historically, Buddha is the name of a radiant leading star that shone for the first time on the horizon of the spiritual world. He with the ample amount of curiosity, probed deep into the mystery of life. Consequently, he realised that life and the world are fraught with sorrows and sufferings. He himself explicitly and reflectively remarks "Luxuries of the palace, healthy bodies, rejoicing youth! What do they mean to me? Pride of youth, pride of health, and pride of existence—all thoughtful people must cast them aside." He further says that dawn is followed by dusk, day by night, happiness by unhappiness, youth by old age, profit by loss, light by darkness, victory by defeat and life by death etc. Remarkably, his philosophy begins with suffering and it is known as the four-fold-judgement:

There is suffering
There is a cause of suffering
There is cessation of suffering
There is a way leading to the cessation of suffering.

Buddha was not only the son but also the boundless joy of king Suddhodan who reigned a vast empire, south of the Himalayas with its capital at Kapilavastu. Mahamaya was his mother. Earlier his name was Siddharatha that stands for the accomplishment of the goal of life. But it is a controversial matter. According to the Purāṇa, Buddha incarnated himself in the vast and ancient country of Kīkat adjacent to Gayā. His virtuous father's name was Ajana.

At the outset of his life, he was immersed in luxurious life to the full but after a while, some incidents opened his mind's eye and then he reverted to the problem of suffering.

In this way, leading the life of renunciation, he started on the eternal quest, that is to say, he set himself to the mission of life–salvation.

It would be very interesting to mention that there lived Asita, a great hermit in the mountain not very far away from Kapilvastu. The hermit prognosticated. "This prince, if he remains in the palace after his youth, will become a great king to rule the four seas. But if he forsakes the worldly life to embrace a religious life, he will become a Buddha and the world's saviour." In the long run, the prediction of paramount importance correspondingly came true and Buddha became the great champion of mankind.

KALKI

Kalki, as the last incarnation of Viṣṇu, one of the most prominent Vedic deities, will behove the world of mortality when darkness, hatred, vices, crimes, sins, dishonesty, theft, robbery, oppression, fraudulence and malpractices sway their power in each and every nook and corner of the whole world. Kalki without doubt, will incarnate himself in order to restore moral, spiritual and religious value. Consequently, there will be the highest amount of expectation of revolutionary changes in every direction. In other words, it is predestined to usher in a new era which will be remarkably known as the Golden Age representing an epoch of righteousness, imperturbability, pity and purity.

Kalki is expected to descend the earth from the paradise by mounting on a strong horse. Sometimes he is shown as having two arms and sometimes four ones. He often appears with a flaming sword in one hand as well as a bridle in the other. As far as his four arms are concerned, he holds a wheel a conch-shell, an arrow and a sword in all of them. It is sanctioned in one of the sacred books that he is horse-headed personality who bears a mace. In this way, he abases and shames Cupid of the Hindu Mythology, the god of love, in the beauty of his appearance. The wheel stands for progress as well as the cycle of life and death; the conch-shell proclaims the glory of saints and monks; the arrow stands for male energy and the power of love; the sword symbolises wisdom and enlightenment; the mace stands for the power of natural laws.

KṚṢṆA IN A DANCING POSE ON A SERPENT

KṚṢṆA IN A DANCING POSE ON A SERPENT

There lived in the black coloured water of the river Yamunā, an evil serpent, Kaliya. The water which used to serve as drinking water was fully polluted and poisoned by the serpent, and consequently whoever drank it, at once paid the debt of nature. At the same time, there was dread and fear in the hearts and minds of the people. Even a large number of birds, animals and insets became extinct. In the meantime, Lord Kṛṣṇa incarnated himself and began chalking out strategies of destroying the hopelessly dangerous snake.

Remarkably, the incarnation of God aims at not only annihilating plenty of giants and demons but also ensuring the well being of mankind.

Kṛṣṇa himself the eighth incarnation of Viṣṇu, climbed a giant tree named Kadamba (*neulea oriental* of which the fruit is eaten) and from there he jumped into the river. Then he started dancing on the hoods of Kaliya which were badly hurt. Thereafter, the water of Yamunā became free of poison. In this way, all the inhabitants of Vraja and the adjoining areas as well as different kinds of creatures felt very delighted.

The snake represents selfishness, brutality and shortcomings which poison the happy source of life. As a matter of fact, the inspiring preaching and teachings by such an incarnation make the source of life physically, morally and spiritually prosperous.

The snake also symbolises a bundle of nerves and Kṛṣṇa stands for the soul that is the main source of life. He has two legs which represent two aspects—bondage and liberty (deliverance). He stretches his two hands—one points to the mortal world or terrestrial one, and the other refers to the next world. In other words, he wants to point out that everything decays with the passage of time with the exception of God. So we should not look only down but also up.

VIṢṆU IN A REPOSING POSE ON A SERPENT-KING

VIṢṆU IN A REPOSING POSE ON A SERPENT-KING

Viṣṇu reclines on a bed of coils of the serpent king. He is omnipotent, omniscient and omnipresent in the world of mortality. Even above him, there remains the one thousand headed Ultimate Reality (Puruṣa) who is worshipped by Viṣṇu and other deities. Puruṣa has occupied the three fourths of the entire cosmos, on the other hand, Viṣṇu has occupied a one fourth portion hereof. He is blue complexioned. Sometimes he is seen with four hands and sometimes more than four. In the first hand, he holds a conch-shell; in the second, he holds a wheel; in the third, he bears a lotus-flower; and the fourth shows the postures of fearlessness and protection but sometimes it is graced with a club. The wheel symbolises the Universal Mind, the constant process of life and death, creation and annihilation. The conch-shell proclaims the glory of saints. The spiral, the interior of the conch-shell signifies infinite space which expands in a clockwise rotation. If its motion is anti-clock-wise, the laws of nature are reverse. It is also the symbol of existence. The club stands for a ritual artefact-power of natural laws and time which destroys everything along its path, symbolically, linked with a lingam and a staff. It is also the symbol of the power of enlightenment as the essence of life. The lotus-flower stands for renunciation. His consort is Lakṣmī and his vehicle is an eagle.

Brahmā sees the light emanating from the navel of Viṣṇu.

According to Hindu Mythology, śeṣa signifies left-over which is seen floating on the ocean. It stands for the universe; śeṣa was also used as a strong rope by the great gods and demons while churning the waters of the ocean. Garuḍa stands for the three Vedas. Symbolically he precludes fraudulence, deception, crookedness. He wears the yellow dress which stands for the earth full of greenery and prosperity.

ŚIVA

ŚIVA

Śiva is the only one essential element that pervades each and every iota of the universe. He is the presiding element. He is the creator, protector and annihilator. In spite of living in the cremation-ground, he is the Lord (adhipati) of the three worlds. Being hidden, he is manifested. Despite being the cause of everything, he is causeless (Akāraṇa). He is given a good name 'Śiva'. The word 'śiva' is synonymous with the God of sovereign power. He abounds with nectar in the form of boundless joy and delight. That is the requirement of each and every creature. This is why, he is credited with the title Śadānanda'. He has two forms: 1. Corporeal 2. Non-corporeal. When he is attached with illusion (Māyā) or possessed of attributes he becomes corporeal form (Saguṇa Brahma), but when he dissociates or separates himself from Māyā, he passes for the non-corporeal (Nirguṇa Brahma).

Śiva is known as Maheśwara when all the three qualities– Sattva-poise, rajas-passion and tamas-stupor of Brahmā. Viṣṇu and Śiva pass into the only one radiant personality, he passes for Maheśvara = Mahā + Īśvara i.e., the Great God. He is said to be Mahāpraṇava or Auṁ, the Almighty. Just as there are seven parts like Akār, Ukār, Maker, Nād, Bindu, Kalā and Kalātīt, in Mahāpraṇava in the same way, Śiva has five manifested faces as well as two hidden ones. This form of his is Praṇava (God, the holy monosyllable).

In the Vedic period, Rudra was considered to be synonymous with Śiva i.e., in his earlier form (Śiva) was called Rudra.

According to Indian Philosophy, he is regarded as the truth, the good and the beauty (Satyam, Śivam and Sundaram). It is believed that there is an abundance of the temples of Amon on the holy banks of the Nile in Egypt as there is an abundance of the temples of Śiva on the banks of the Ganges in India.

He represents destruction, austerity as well as the comparatively malignant forces of life. He is benevolent and malevolent. The ideas of creation and destruction are found closely combined in one of his aspects as the Ultimate Reality (Mahādeva).

Remarkably, he is known by the three names–Śiva, Śambhū and Śankar that are very popular throughout the world. On the ground of a volley of questions and answers, he has been extolled to the heavens at a number of places. There are lots of Upaniṣadas but one of them—Māṇḍukya concludes only with the glorification and extolment of śiva. When Śankara plays the role of an annihilator, his vehicle is a lion. During the Dooms Day, he bears the epithet 'Rudra' and the corpse works as his vehicle.

Śiva is of fair complexion. He is blessed with the trinity of eyes. He has long sacred and matted hair. His head is crowned with the sacred Gaṅgā and the crescent moon. His neck, head and arms are decked with the numerous serpents and rudrākṣa. His throat has turned blue because of having drunk the greatest amount of venom. He is two armed. In one hand, he has a rosary called rudrākṣa. The other has the expression of blessing. Sometimes he is shown having four arms. Two hands give blessing and protective expressions. Either of the other two hands holds a trident and the drum namely a ḍamaru (a particular kind of drum). He is always seen in the state of nature. The whole of his body is besmeared with ash. He wears tiger-skin.

A wreath of skulls adorns his neck. Pārvatī is his consort. He has two sons-Gaṇeśa and Kārtikeya. The bull which is known as Nandi is his vehicle. A rosary signifies unity in diversity and its vacuum for cosmos. The Gaṅgā represents knowledge; this is the reason that she is called Jāhnavi. She also stands for a particular sort of fluid of one thousand petalled lotus. The moon stands for soma (ambrosia). The bull symbolises religion (dharma) and its four legs stand for penance, cleanliness, mercy and charity. Vilvapatra which symbolises the heart and its three leaves stand for the three attributes of nature—raj, sat and tam. The drum stands for the primal sound, the inception of the universe and also the rhythm, vibration and the strength of the cosmos. It is also a part of paraphernalia used in ritual worship. The trident is the symbol of the three attributes of God: creation, preservation and destruction. A conch proclaims the glory of saints, the spiral interior of the conch shell signifies infinite space which moves in a clockwise rotation. Supposing its motion is anti-clock-wise, the laws of nature are reversed.

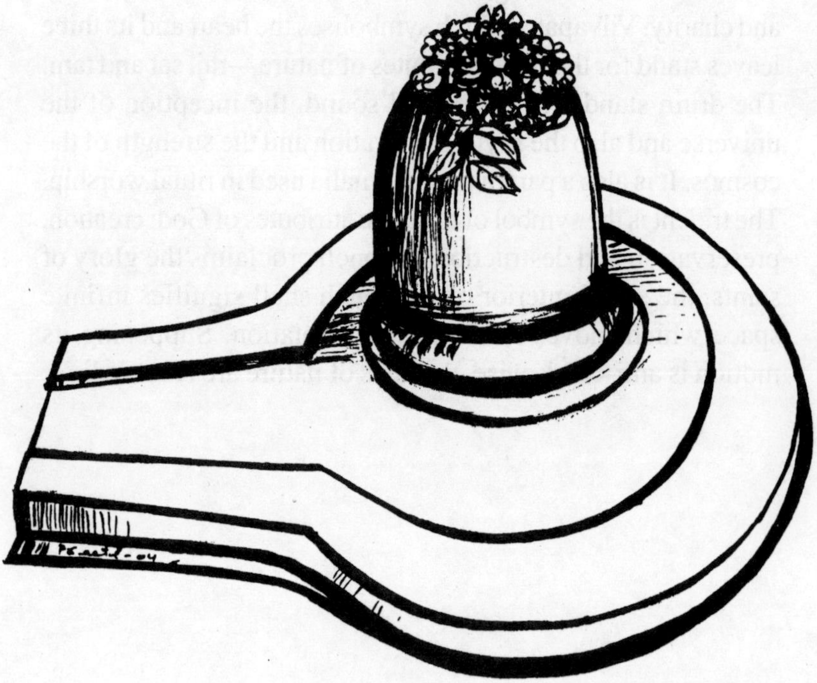

ŚIVALIṄGA (PHALLUS)
A Historical Background

Since time out of mind, Śivaliṅga (an image of the erect penis of Lord Śiva as a symbol of generative and creative energy) was prevalent not only in the orient courtiers but also in the occident ones. The scriptures of Rome and Greece speak volumes for the worship of the Phallus. In Egypt, a deity named Osirih is considered to be the presiding deity of the river, Nile. In the ancient Chinese and Japanese literatures, the phallus-adoration finds expression. The fifteenth chapter of the old testament of the Bible refers to the pillar of fire resembling the liṅga. This sort of idol-worship led to a cult which came to be known as phallicism. Sir John Marshall is of the opinion that Śaivadharma refers to Chalcolithic age or the prehistorical age.

On the other hand, In India, the worshipping of the phallus had already been introduced in the remote past. In accordance with Śiva Purāṇa and other religious scriptures counting in the excavation of Mohan Jodaro, some significant strings of information surface that of yore, people used to worship the liṅga and its continuity had not shattered even then.

The liṅga is vertically carved out of stone in a general way. This structure consists of tri-part. The base is square with a pedestal. Herein a vertical round shaped stone is installed.

The sky is considered to be the phallus; the earth is its background and the remaining portions are said to be those of the great deities. According to the etymological meaning of Saṁskṛta term "Liṅga" everything animate or inanimate is merged into it, this is why it is called liṅga. Even in the age of science, a mathematician of international repute has demonstrated that the blue unknown firmament is a curve which is the form of liṅga. Time, space and matter are said to be the liṅga where from the entire world is created. In other words, a straight line does not have existence without a curve.********

The penis and the vagina (liṅga and yoni) are the primal mysteries of the creation. There is no possibility of the creation without the combination of Prakṛti and Puruṣa or the coition of male and female organs. It also consists of sattva (the preponderance of Sattva renders one contemplative, righteous self-denying and benevolent); rajas (just Rajas leads him to lead life full of quick and energetic activity); and tamas (Tamas gives rise to evil passion and bad thoughts, ignorance, vanity, greed). Grains like wheat, barley sprout in a particular portion of a plant and the very portion is called vagina.

Śiva and śakti, God and illusion or mysterious power (Māyā), Puruṣa and Prakṛti are initial cause of the creation. According to Tantraśāstra, the vagina is said to be triangular and the penis central. There arises no question of separation of their close relation. According to the scriptures, there are different types of phalluses which run thus:

1. Gandhaliṅga
2. Puṣpaliṅga
3. Goṣkariliṅga
4. Rajomayaliṅga
5. Yavagodhumashalijaliṅga
6. Sitakhaṇḍamaya liṅga
7. Lavanajaliṅgas and what not

PAÑCAMUKHA ŚIVA

That Lord Śiva has one face is widely known throughout the world, but he is also five faced. This is the reason that he passes for Pañcānana, Pañcamukha and Pañcavaktra (epithets of śiva). These five ones are dealt with thus—the first resembles an elephant (pearl), this particular kind of gem is supposed to be found in the head of elephants (Gajamuktā). It is light red in colour; the second is yellow coloured; the third is the blue complexioned face which takes after a handsome patch of a cloud containing water; the fourth is of grey colour and like diamond; the fifth is sanguine (thick blood coloured) and like a flower, namely, Javā. These are known as Akār (Tattapurṣ) Akār or Aghora, Makāra, Nāda and Bindu. The first face refers to Brahmā, the second to Viṣṇu, the third to Rudra, the fourth Iśvara and the fifth refers to Maheśvara. They are also called God, the holy monosyllable. He is the possessor of the three eyes and each of his faces is graced with the moon as well as a blue coloured crown. The nimbus of crores of his visages like the full moon beggars description. The marvellous glimpse into this happy sight fills lots of the hearts with joy unspeakable. He holds a trident, a battleaxe (paraśu), a sword, a thunder-bolt (Vajra), fire, a serpent-king, a bell, a lasso, posture of fearlessness. He is a well wisher. He is a benevolent and munificent deity like Kalpataru—the tree of Indra's paradise (It is such a tree as yields anything we desire).

All of his faces epitomise the five primal elements out of which the world and the human body are composed. They stand for the five major deities like Gaṇeśa, Sūrya (the sun), Viṣṇu, Śiva and Ādiśakti Durgā. They also symbolise the five worlds, namely, hell, earth, the world of the manes or the deceased ancestors, the world of deities celestial sphere and paradise. Fire refers to the fire of the stomach that helps to digest food. They are also expressive of earth, fire, water, air and ether.

LORD ŚIVA, THE MENDICANT

Lord Śiva, the greatest donor of the whole world, is the third god of the Hindu triad. He is also known as the Lord of cremation-grounds. He represents annihilation, penance and malignant forces of life. It is an astoundingly paradoxical matter that being the donor, he tends to play the role of a mendicant excellently. In order to have the proper understanding of the context, we think over it in two ways-first he appears to be an ordinary beggar performing the cosmic play for the good and welfare of man-kind. He mumps and craves Annapūrṇā, the great goddess, for the vital air (Prāṇa), the heart, wisdom and various varieties of corns.

Remarkably, by the way of his activity, he demonstrates to the world that not only he but all the individual souls are humbly asking her for something or the other.

In this way, he maintains the close relation between the donor and the beggar, which carries paramount significance at the time of creation as well as annihilation. The goddess, an embodiment of energy, always empowers him to retain the process of creation.

ŚIVA NAṬARĀJA

Lord Śiva assumes various popular forms–sometimes the fascinating and sometimes awfully formidable. His posture is beyond words when he stages a particular kind of dance which is known as "Tāṇḍava'–a violent dance. In the Gupta-period, there is a mention of a great dancer (Mahānata that is closely referred to Śiva). It is traditionally acknowledged that he introduced dance and stage craft. For the manifestation of a definite event or matter, the limbs of the body are put to action or operation, which is called the act of dancing (Nāṭya or Nāṭana). He is a prime dancer. Because of showing reverence for the glory of the act of dancing, he is called Naṭarāja that is his ancient epithet. The entire cosmos is his theatre. With the movement of his body—his dance—the world is put to action. When the act of dancing ceases, the sentient and lifeless world is engrossed in peace and delight of the Supreme Soul.

All the activities of God are reflected in the dance performed by Naṭarāja. The symbolism of Tāṇḍava can be dealt with in a number of ways. It represents the moving force of the universe. At the same time, it also refers to creation, preservation, annihilation, embodiment as well as deliverance which symbolise the five acts of God. Pāṇinī, the most accomplished and celebrated Hindu grammarian and saint who composed Aṣṭādhyāyī, the famous treatise on Sanskrit grammar, has implemented and pronounced fourteen formulas such as

1. AIUṆ	2. ṚLṚK
3. EOṄ	4. AI AU C
5. HA YA VA RA T	6. LAṆ
7. ÑA MA ṄA ṆA NA M	8. JHA BHA Ñ
9. GHA ḌHA DHA Ṣ	10. JA BA GA ḌA DAŚ
11. KHA PHA CHA THA THA CA TA TA V	12. KA PA Y
13. ŚA ṢA SA R	14. HA L.

These are the product of the sounds of the drum (ḍamarū) of Lord Shiva. There is an interesting story about Śiva who being in the comfortable and cosy company of Viṣṇu started tormenting ten thousand religious men. They were dwelling in a jungle. They got out of temperament and sent an awful tiger to Śiva but he put it to death and ornamented his body with its skin. Hereafter, they sent him a serpent which he garlanded himself. Again they sent a pygmy on which he began dancing following which they acknowledged their defeat. In accordance with Śivāgama, there are seven kinds of symbolism of dance—Ānanda Tāṇḍava, Sādhytāṇḍava, Kālikatāṇḍava, Saṁhārtāṇḍava, Umātāṇḍava, Tripuratāṇḍava and Gauriṭāṇḍava. It is also worth mentioning that on the occasion of Sāndhyatāṇḍava Brahma plays the tabor (Mṛdaṅga); Saraswati plays the Veeṇā (an Indian instrument like a lute); Indra blows the flute; Viṣṇu beats the drum and Lakṣmī sings a song and all the gods enjoy dancing.

Śiva holds the drum in the first hand, in the second, fire, the third shows protecting expression, and the fourth betokens one of his feet. The pigmy symbolises ignorance. His first foot stands for deliverance and enlightenment. The drum is the symbol of the Nāda-Brahma, the sound Brahma. Fire stands for the annihilation of the universe. His feet characterise the shelter of the individual souls.

THE MARRIAGE PROCESSION OF LORD ŚIVA

Marriage is an extremely sacred sacrament that persists through the world wide. Especially in India, it has been underlined by a galaxy of monks and writers since the dawn of civilization. Even at present, it has not lost its importance and value. Lots of significant books on sacraments have been brought out e.g. Manusmṛṭi, Bhṛgusaṁhitā and Purāṇas. Now we come to the main point. An admirable preparation for the marriage procession of Lord Śiva has been finalised. This is a unique type of marriage procession which is accompanied by different kinds of characters. Some are gods like Brahmā, Viṣṇu and what not. Some are ghosts, goblins and witches having different visages. Some of them are physically handicapped; some are smartly dressed but some are also found in the state of nature. In this way, in the company of the aforesaid figures, he himself has assumed an astoundingly fearful appearance with all his equipment. In the light of these facts, it is the best and the most relevant device to discover the psychology of this bride (the would be consort) counting in all the members of her family. Only then the concept of might have materialised of the permanence of marriage is maintained.

Indeed his marriage represents the good and the evil, the rich and the poor, the intelligent and the fool, nectar and poison, introversion and extroversion. Meaning thereby is that nothing should be discarded.

HANUMĀNA

HANUMĀNA

Hanumāna is the name of a deity. He is celebrated and prominent as a monkey-god whose sublime and lustrous appearance finds expression in the Rāmāyaṇa to the most possible extent. According to the Vedas, Upaniṣadas and Purāṇas, he himself is regarded as the Supreme Being. He is endowed with great divine power as Rudra. He is the embodiment of AUM and is subject to adoration. He assumed the most powerful appearance for the accomplishment and completion of Śṛ Rāma's mission. He is the storehouse of unlimited power, knowledge, learning and enlightenment. He is the eleventh incarnation of God Śiva. Remarkably, Śiva and Viṣṇu worship each other incessantly. But when Viṣṇu assumed the incarnation, Śiva also incarnated himself as Hanumāna He is known as a messenger of God (Rāma).

He is the son of Pavan (Wind-God). Why he is called Hanumāna excites our curiosity that can be quenched on the basis of the etymological analysis of the word. 'Hanumāna' is derived from the root word 'Hanu'. After fixing a suffix 'matup', we have the formation of this word, which signifies queerness.

His sacred life aims at devoting his excellent services in this vast creation. His appearance refers to 'Makār' which is synonymous with Śiva. The lusture of his appearance is yellow complexioned like dropping lightning. Remarkably, he assumes various forms: sometimes mammoth and sometimes minute. He is called Bajaraṅga (having a very stout and strong body like a thunder-bolt). Vālmīki has dished up the same picture of Hanumāna, through the Rāmāyaṇa, the most ancient epic of the world. Sometimes he is depicted as having the appearance of a monkey and sometimes he assumes a human form. It has been borne out even by the Adhyātma Rāmāyaṇa. He is also produced as a physician. Sometimes he disguises himself as Vipra and sometimes he is shown as Vaṭu, an anchorite, a monk and what not.

There is a clear depiction of the different colours of his body but indisputably, he is represented as golden complexioned. His body is graced with vermillion. It is very interesting to mention that the shadow of his body measures thirty yojans by ten yojanas (a yojana is a measure of distance, roughly thirteen kilo metres). He has one head, and two hand: one holds a mace and the other a mountain. He possesses a very large and long tail which loops over his enormous head. The front portion of this tail is like a coral. It looks like a flag. His hair is of tawny colour. He wears ear-rings. It is quite difficult to see his face in the dazzling light. His shoulders are strong and broad, and his waist is thin and slender. The line of his hairs extending across the navel is thick. The lips are small. The colour of his tongue and face is like that of copper. His ears are red coloured. Inside the wide open mouth, there are white coloured teeth. According to Nāradīya Purāṇa, his face is rose-coloured. His fist has importance as a fearful weapon. But his nail does not have less value. He has two legs which are very strong. It is worth mentioning that he does not have any vehicle as he is fully confident of his physical, mental and spiritual power. Our scriptures point out to the fact that no one can be put in comparison with his strength and speed in the whole world. The mace is a ritual artifact representing the power of natural laws and time which destroys everything along its path. The big round shaped portion of the mace is the head of the human body and its staff stands for the spinal chord. The fist stands for the unlimited power of the five elements such as earth, water, fire, air and ether. The tail is the symbol of Kuṇḍalinī Śakti (Serpentine energy). The mountain signifies calamities and difficulties which are removed by Hanumāna. This is the reason that he is called Saṁkaṭa Mocana.

PAÑCAMUKHA HANUMĀNA

This is the singularly the divine form of Hanumāna who is blessed with the five faces. He appears very fearful. He possesses fifteen eyes and ten arms and is capable of removing various hurdles and obstacles. He fulfils all the desires of mankind. The first face is that of a monkey. This is gifted with the lusture of crores of suns. The second refers to the face of a man and a lion (Nṛsiṁha—the fourth incarnation of Viṣṇu). This is the marvellous form which dispels fear and dread. The body with this face is fraught with the dazzling light. The third refers to an eagle (Garuḍa) which alleviates all types of ailments and maladies. The fourth points to the face of a boar. A man is relieved of fever with the help of this appearance. The fifth refers to the face of a horse. This appearance destroys demons. His eyes are of yellowish colour. His head is graced with a crown and is clothed in yellow. He is ornamented with the different weapons such as—nails, a tail, limbs, a tooth, a trident and a sword a goad, a mountain, a pillar, a fist, a mace, and a branch of a tree.

MALE DEITIES

BHAIRAVA

Bhairava, the fifth incarnation of Lord Śiva, is singularly the deity of tantras. The former is the destructing power of the latter. Yogis termed it as Bhairo Cakra (Plexus). Assuming the form of a dog, the Lord of Death (Yamarāja) himself discharges orders issued by him and in this way, the complicated process of life and death goes on till eternity.

The meaning of Bhairava—the word 'Bhairava' signifies awful so it is up to the mark to call him Rudra. He sways his power over death (Kāla). One analysis, Kāla = K+ā+la; K stands for ākāś bīj, ā for Pṛthvī bīj and la for Bhairava bīj i.e. the space between the earth and the sky is considered to be kāla Bhairo.

According to Āgama, he is also called the dark night. In Skandapurāṇa, there is the description of the origin of Kālabhairo. Just as Śṛ Rāma and Kṛṣṇa incarnated themselves on the earth to annihilate demons, in the same way, Śiva incarnated himself as Bhairo to humble Brahmā's pride.

According to scriptures, there are one thousand eight Bhairavas. Again in the eyes of an accomplisher (sādhaka), he is called by one hundred and eight names. Eight of them were appointed as the Koṭawāla (police chief) of Kāśī.

Śwan (dog) is known as the vehicle of Bhairo. Its olfactory power (smelling capacity) is very strong, and has great detective power. Even scientists have recently put a dog to use to ascertain the position of the numerous planets in the unknown blue sky. This dog bears the name 'Laika' which was sent into the second satellite launched by Russia. 'Śwan' does not purport a dog but such an animal as is intelligent, quick-witted, faithful and dutiful.

Bhairo is fraught with mercy, dutifulness and delight. Sometimes he is two handed and sometimes four or eight. He holds a staff, a small bell and an ornament which is worn round the ankles. He has also a broom which stands for the purification of the heart. He is garlanded with the skulls which symbolise alphabet. One of his hands is armed with the drum (ḍamarū) that stands for 'Nād Bindu'. He has also a trident which represents cough, bile and gout or rheumatism. He holds a snake which signifies one of the prominent ganglions in the body (Kuṇḍalinī). The begging skull is used by him to ask Annapūrṇā for alms. He possesses a tail which stands for valour and bravery. When all colours are blended, a new one i.e. black colour comes to light: the point where a form is merged into a shapeless one and the point where time and space are mingled. Darkness is said to be the real form of Kāla Bhairo. The same Bīja Mantra of Bhairo and Kālī is K. The following diagram gives us a fair idea about the different Bhairavas.

Aṣṭa Bhairo	Prapañca		Śakti (Power)	Diśā (Direction)	Bīja mantra Vedic hymns in form of a seed
Asitāṅga	Bhīṣaṇa	Ḍākanī	Bhrāhmī	East	An
Ruru	Kalarāja	Devī	Maheśvarī	South-East	In
Candra	Saṁhāraka	Hākinī	Kaumārī	South	Un
Krodha	Ruru	Yākinī	Vaiṣṇavī	West-South	Ri
Unmat	Unmat	Lākinī	Vārāhī	West	Lrin
Kapālī	Krodha	Śākinī	Indrāṇī	North-west	En
Bhīṣaṇa	Candrakapāla	Rākinī	Cāmuṇḍā	North	On
Saṁhār	Bhūtanātha	Kākinī	Mahālakṣmī	North East	Ah

VIŚVAKARMĀ

Viśvakarmā, the presiding deity of all craftsmen, is the cre ator of the entire universe. He is the indicative of gigantic force. He is of white complexion. His head is crowned, and has a white beard. He is embellished with various sorts of ornaments. He is four handed. All of them hold a scripture, a lasso, a water-pot, a craftsman's tool. His vehicle is an elephant.

In accordance with scriptures, he is unique and peerless in the sphere of art, science and architecture. He occupies the most important position among all deities. He is regarded as the first engineer and scientist. For example, he has built different kinds of the flying chariots of the gods. The weapons and the instruments of trade were his creations.

Remarkably, a religious sacrifice was performed by him wherein he offered not only himself but also all creatures in order to give a potent interpretation pertaining to the cyclic process of annihilation as well as the renewal of mind (cosmic life) and matter.

The cities of Lankā and Dvārkā were also built by him. The former belongs to Rāvaṇa, the demon-king, and the latter belongs to Lord Kṛṣṇa as it is sanctioned in the sacred books. The four hands stand for the four ages of Hindu mythology Satya (the golden-age); Dvāpara (the silver-age); Tretā (the copper-age); and Kali (the iron age). His beard symbolises something endowed with goodness and virtuousness

(Sātvikatā). The water contained in the vase stands for existence. The book is the symbol of the store-house of spiritual knowledge. The lasso stands for attachment of the mundane and also the capacity of god to capture evil and ignorance. The elephant represents gravity and profundity.

KĀRTIKEYA

Kārtikeya, the elder brother of god Gaṇeśa, is the com mander of deities. He is said to be the god of war. He is famous for his unlimited power. He is in the capacity of subduing and suppressing the men of demoniac bent of mind. At the same time, he commands the forces in order to surmount difficulties and obstacles and to defend mankind. He is gifted with the divine power. Remarkably, when he was appointed to the post of the general of the army of the gods, a number of deities offered him different sorts of things. Viṣṇu offered him a divine weapon to wage a war; the god of fire blessed him with effulgence and brilliance. The god of air provided him with a peacock as a vehicle.

He has six heads and four arms. His hands are armed with prongs or goads. A garland of crystal becomes his neck. His vehicle is a peacock which is an elegantly charming bird.

As for as Kārtikeya's origin in concerned, there are a lot of references in the Vedas and the Purāṇas etc. According to Śiva Purāṇa, in order to kill great demons like Tārak etc., a host of deities offered prayers to Lord Śiva. No sooner did he grant their prayers than a certain amount of semen dropped off the head onto the earth. It was swallowed by Fire (Agnideva) as a pigeon on an impetus or impulse of the deities. On being enraged at his action, Pārvatī inflicted a curse on him comprising the deities. They began to lead their life in great agony. As a result, the six wives of Ursa Major, the Great Bear (the Indian Peiales) became pregnant and began to pass through a sorry plight. They by discarding semen, they cast it into the flow of the Gaṅgā. As soon as the (Gaṅgā) discarded it in the forest of reeds, a child was born. He bore the name of Kārtikeya.

According to the first poet, Vālmīki, Swāmi Kārtikeya is born from the galaxy. The Gaṅgā discarded her conception (womb). Hereafter when he appeared and magnified his personality, six Kritikas presented themselves to suckle him milk.

According to Astrology, there are six stars in all under Kṛtika, a sidereal name, in the azure unknown sky. Being brought up by Kṛtikas, a blessed son came to be known as Ṣaḍānana or Kārtikeya.

The peacock multi-coloured, natural and graceful creature, is the focus of attraction. Five works of art are painted on its feathers. It is not born in the process of coitus i.e., it is beyond the enjoyment of sex. It is discernible that during the rainy season, being heavily intoxicated, it begins to dance and all of a sudden, discharges semen on the earth. It is swallowed by a pea-hen and then it becomes pregnant.

In accordance with the Purāṇas, Kārtikeya came to being by means of the discharge of semen.

Just as the peacock does not get affected even after swallowing the numerous serpents, in the same fashion, he swallows or stomachs demons, devils, giants, sinners and tyrants.

His six heads represent the six scriptures (Śāśtras) as well as the six plexuses. The four hands refer to the four directions and to four ages. The peacock stands for joviality, beauty and popularity.

KUBERA

Kubera, the god of inexhaustible wealth and legendary trea sure-house, is the custodian deity of the Northern direction. He is also reputed to be Yakṣa Raj who resides at Alakāpurī (the city of god Kubera) situated on a peak of the Himalayas. He is of white complexion. His face wears gloominess. He is a dwarf (undersized) and ugly. He has three legs as well as eight teeth. Ever and anon he is two handed and several times he is four handed. The middle part of his body is protruding. He carries different items in all of his hands such as a fruit, a vase, a mace, a bowl and a purse full of money. He is insipid in nature and voice. The external parts of his body are decked with ornaments. He has a very beautiful garden called Caitraratha situated on mount Mandra where Nature herself has strewn all her wealth.

His mind is always centred on money and wealth. Sometimes he is seen with a wine-pot. He has a chariot which is pulled by men.

Being indifferent to religion and knowledge as well as having extreme vanity and pride in his wealth and property, he is involved and embroiled in a quagmire of materialism. At some places, he is shown boarded on an aeroplane embellished with flowers. Basically, he is the treasurer of the great goddess Lakṣamī. He deals out wealth and money only to those aspir-

ants that really deserve in conformity with the order issued by her. He is also said to be demon-king Rāvaṇa's brother.

It is worth mentioning that he (Rāvaṇa) had snatched the kingdom of Lankā, the aeroplane, wealth and property from him (Kubera).

Being a strong supporter of materialism, he is cursed with ugliness, deformity, narrow-mindedness, poorness and wrong deeds. In spite of holding an exalted position and rank, he does not merit admiration. Considering the flaws in his character it is worth taking a note of this suggestive and memorable fact that grace as well as beauty comes out of sacrament, good conduct and gentle behaviour. These are the things which he lacks. The bellying out of his stomach is expressive of discontent or dissatisfaction. The amassing of more and more wealth and money signifies that the real soul has been mortgaged in the hands of materialism. In this way, it is an explicit message to mankind that real life consists in contentment and meekness but not in wealth. The collection of money causes hatred like excreta full of foul odour. His eight teeth stand for eight accomplishments (Siddhis).

NĀRADA

Like the world of mortality, there also exists the marvellous abode of gods wherein a constellation of sages dwell. Nārada is one of them who has devoted and dedicated his life to the adoration of God and to inspire the individual souls to follow the path of truth and righteousness. Being the seer of some hymns of the Ṛg Veda, he assumed the third incarnation as Devarṣi Nārada. He is a recluse and blessed with the grace of the Ultimate Reality. Being a profoundly knowledgeable character, he is adroit and adept in the Vedas and the Upaniṣads etc. He is the central figure in the universe. He is the leading guide of those who are very inquisitive to enjoy salvation as well as commune with God. He is one of the ten sons born in accordance with the Purāṇs by wish not by coition.

According Viṣṇu Purāṇa, he is considered to be the son of Dakṣa's daughter. He is the inventor of the Vīṇā (the Indian lute).

On analysis, 'Nārada' consists of two 'words': Nāra+Da. The former stands for knowledge and the latter for giver, that is to say, one who imparts knowledge as well information to the people with weal and welfare in view. Even according to scriptures, he imparts knowledge with respect to God.

On the contrary, in our conservative society, people normally consider him to be such a figure who causes dispute. But it sounds wide of the mark.

He passes for a divine sage. By appearance, he is more handsome, and lustrous than Cupid. One of his hands is equipped with the Vīṇā. The other one and his neck are charmingly garlanded. He is fidgety or fickle-minded. All the time, he utters Nārāyaṇa-Nārāyaṇa (the name of God). He is of keen intellect, endowed with vim and profound knowledge. He conveys a relevant string of advice and sermon to a galaxy of deities, sages, hermits and diabolic-devilish natured figures at the appropriate place and the suitable time without being summoned and invoked.

To sum up, he can be called the minister for information and broadcasting on the ground of the role played by him throughout the tri-world. His two hands symbolize the two central forces Nara and Nārāyaṇ (the soul and God), Śiva and Śakti, Prakṛti and Puruṣa.

DHANVANTARI

Since the outset of the universe, the conspicuously impor tant medical science has been in existence. It has been universally acknowledged especially by means of scriptures, (Hindu Mythology) that India is well known for numerous types of her pathies. Āyurveda is one of them. It is the most ancient pathy throughout the world and hereafter many other pathies came into light through the sincere efforts of various men of letters. First of all, Dhanvantari, the most scholarly figure, is profoundly proficient in the medical surgery.

According to Garuḍa Purāṇa, on the occasion of the churning of the ocean, Viṣṇu himself incarnated as Dhanvantari having black-complexioned appearance. He had a divine vase brimming with nectar. He is four handed. The first has a book on Ayurveda, the second a conch-shell, the third a vase containing nectar and the fourth medicinal plants (herbs). After the distribution of nectar, he was appointed as the physician of deities.

He bears different names–Ādideva, Amaravara, Amṛtayoni and Abja. It is said the Dhanvantari is not one but many, such as Kaśirāja, Divodāsa, Aśvanikumāra, Nakula and Sahadeva.

Vikramāditya, well reputed for his judgment throughout the world in the time immemorial, had nine gems. Of them, Dhanvantari, held a sublime position. He is put in comparison

आयुर्वेद

with Lukamāna whose happy and comfortable abode was located in Greece.

Keeping in mind the actual meaning of Āyurveda—the science of knowledge—the combination of physical body, senses, psyche and soul is called 'Āyu' (age) and Veda stands for knowledge—Dhanvantari prepared a divine medicine like ambrosia by having the reasonable proportion of ingredients. After doing a brown study of Āyurveda, the categorised it into eight classic parts which are known as 'Aṣṭāṅga-Āyurveda' =

Śalya	(Surgery)
Śālakya	(Ophthalmology, Otology, Rhinology, Dentistry, Oropharyngology etc.)
Kāya Chikitsā	(Medicine)
Bhūtavidyā	(Psychiatry, Microbiology)
Kaumāra–Bhṛtya	(Paediatrics)
Agadatantra	(Txicology, Medical jurisprudence)
Rasāyana tantra	(Science of rejuvenation, immunology)
Vājīkaraṇa	(Science of aphrodisiac)

He gave a miraculous direction as well as dimension to medical science on a wide scale by propounding 'Dhanvantari Saṁhitā' for the welfare of the world.

The vase represents wisdom, elixir of immortality. The conch-shell stands for the glory of saints. The interior hereof signifies infinite space which expands in a clock-wise rotation. If its motion is anti-clock-wise, the laws of nature will be reversed.

HAYAGRĪVA

Hayagrīva, in the world of mortality, rose to eminence as the incarnation of Viṣṇu of the most exalted position in the midst of the Vedic deities. In order to restore religious, moral and spiritual values and ensure the security and safety of the Vedas and devotee, he assumed this divine and magnificent appearance on the earth. He is handsome and fair complexioned, and has unlimited power. The neck and the visage of his are just like a horse. His pious face resembling a lotus-flower bestows shelter to the Vedas. The star-spangled sky is his head. His hair glows like the silver rays of the moon. The sky as well as the underground are his ears. The earth is his forehead. The Gaṅgā and the Saraswati rivers are his haunch and two seas are his eye-brows. The sun and the moon are his twin eyes. The evening is his nose; Oṁ, the mysterious syllable called the Praṇava, indicative of the various attributes of the Supreme Being; his ornament and lightning is his tongue; manes are his teeth. Brahmaloka, the eternal residence of the great God, Brahmā, is his lips. Kālarātri (the night of annihilation) is his throat. He is beyond beginning and end.

BALRĀMA

Balarāma is an excellent and magnificent incarnation of God. This incarnation represents a new era. The Vedas, in this regard, say that he incarnates himself with a view to ridding the entire earth of a lot of problems like oppression, tyranny, anarchy, lawlessness, fraudulence, dishonesty. By nature, he is earnest and peaceful. In appearance, he is the embodiment of beauty that is beyond world. He has two hands which hold a club or a plough. But occasionally, he is seen with both of them.

Kṛṣṇa and Balarāma are the brothers who are believed to have incarnated themselves at the same time. They also play the role of intimate friends throughout their life by cooperating each other in order to achieve the same goal.

Remarkably, Viṣṇu, the Supreme Being, picked two out of his hairs, one black and the other white and placed them into the pure womb of Devakī and consequently, the two sons were born. They were named Kṛṣṇa as well as Balarāma. The former is of black complexion and the latter is of white one.

As far as the cosmic play is concerned, Kṛṣṇa has to play a major role whereas Balarāma has to play a minor one. The club represents the power of natural laws. The plough stands for intellect, power, bliss, prosperity, the triumph of godly power over demonic one.

KĀMADEVA

There lies truth in the fact that sex is considered to be the starting point of love and the root of life. Scientifically, sex is the energy of tremendous importance which leads animate and inanimate objects to the vast and inner ocean of love. If sex is the nadir, love is the zenith viz. love is the transformation of sex which is represented by Cupid, the well-revered god of not only sex but also of the venerable men of the yogic power. On the one hand, he pierces the soft hearts of creatures by means of his tipped shafts; on the other hand, he, being in hilarious spirits, frees the mind from desires. Many men of letters are of the opinion that spring is the incarnation of Kāmadeva, who assumes the godly and golden appearance which is very graceful and charming. He wears five clothes and ornaments. He is generally two handed but sometimes four ones and sometimes eight ones. He holds a conch-shell, a lotus-flower and magnificent bow and arrows made of the fragrant flowers. These weapons (bow and arrows) are regarded as Kusumākar and Kusumāyudha. Occasionally, his bow is made of sugarcane. He possesses the five flower-tipped shafts of desires to please and infatuate each and every creature of the entire world.

He is always adolescent. His body is besmeared with something extracted from a species of Shrika, the plant *Verbesina calendulacca* and something from a piece of sandal.

His neck is garlanded with the fragrant flowers *Michelia Champacca*. He has four wives named Rati, Prīti, Śakti and Vibhadaśakti. Mostly, he spends his time in the happy and comfortable company of his dearest consort Rati. The parrot works as his vehicle. Even the twin nipples of the breasts of a beautiful and lustful lady play the role of his vehicle.

On the analysis of Kāmadeva, 'Kāma' stands for sex and 'Deva' for god. He is not visible to the naked eyes but his presence is felt everywhere. In the absence hereof, the world will be of no existence.

When the idea of the solitary Supreme Being's self-amorous dalliance came to light, sex-desire struck upon his mind and he, then and there, resolved to assume various appearances in order to create the different worlds and numerous sorts of creates by virtue of this deity.

The presiding deity of sex is Cupid. Mind is the fountain of desire which is represented by him, so he is called Mansija. He is said to be "Manmatha" because of having the attribute of churning all the minds of the whole universe. He is also reputed to be the 'Son of Resolution' because sex emanates from resolution. Sex is a pair of man and woman. It runs through the different parts of the body especially in the legs, the ankle-bone, the temples, the anus, the hearts, the forehead, the navel, the throat, the thigh, the eyes, the lips and the hair of the head.

His five arrows represent a Tāntrik process of killing a person through the influence of mantras, hindrance, yawning, exploitation, and intoxication.

YAMA

YAMA

"Where there is life there is death" is a proverbial sen tence. It is a universal fact that every creature leads to the inevitable hour. In the real sense of the term, Yama, directly and closely refers to death, this is why he is reputed to be the Lord of Death. But he also plays another important role of Dharmarāj (in the guise of the judge of men). Hence it is a dual role by him. As the presiding deity of hell, he is Yama. He holds a distinguished position among the guardians of the eight worlds. He is represented as having green complexion. He is very dreadful in appearance. He is dressed in red. His head is seen ornamented with a crown and a flower. Sometimes he is two handed and sometimes four handed. He holds four weapons such as a pen, a book, a cock and a staff according to Matsya Purāṇa. Ever and anon he is also adorned with a conch-shell, a wheel, a mace and lotus–flower as Viṣṇu, but as Yama, he holds a thunder-bolt. He is seated on a black buffalo.

As a record-keeper, popularly known as Citragupta, Yama is reputed to be a force that does not come from outside but emanates from the sun, the eye of heaven. This personified force alienates the sun from the age of a being resulting there from (the sun). He assumes different forms to the Virtuous and the sinners respectively. He manifests himself as Viṣṇu having the face wearing gleeful and blessed smile. His eyes resemble a lotus-flower. As far as the vicious or sinners are concerned, he is dressed in leather like a thundering cloud expressive of devastation appears before them. The Virtuous are sent to heaven and the sinners to hell.

Significantly, those who are not acquainted with the scientific language like Sanskrit, no doubt, fail to discriminate between Yama, the deity and Yama, a historical personage.

He bears various names-excluding the aforesaid Pitṛpati, Samavartī, Paretarat, Kṛtānta, Yamunābhrātā, Śamana, Kala, Dandadhara, Śrāddhadeva, Vaivasvat, Anataka, Jīviteśa, Mahaṣidhvaja, Auḍambara, Kīnāśa, Śīrṇapāda, Kanka, Bhīmaśāsana, Mahiṣa-vāhana etc.

The book stands for spiritual knowledge, the wheel for completion, enlightenment and life-death. The conch-shell signifies the space which expands in a clock-wise rotation. If its motion is anti-clock-wise, the constant laws of nature are reversed. The mace stands for the power of laws made by the divine authority for the proper regulation of society or for correct conduct in life. The lotus is the symbol of mystical power, joy, beauty, purity and eternal renewal. The thunder-bolt stands for intuition and wisdom. The buffalo represents ignorance, insensate objects and indiscretion.

PROVISION OF LAWS FOR HARSH PUNISHMENT FOR SINS

Evil deeds result in sorry plight and predicament. Passions bring man to disgrace and destruction. These can be put in comparison with that which causes weal in the beginning but woe in the end. The world itself is fraught with merit and demerit, joy and sorrow. So it is but natural that there will be two types of men herein, the virtuous as well as the vicious. In this way, those who commit sins or infringe God's laws lead to damnation undergoing the tortures of hell which has been conveniently and remarkably categorised into eighty six infernal-ponds which are despairingly hideous and formidable in their structure and nature. They are as hideous and formidable pits (Kundas) which run thus:

Vahni, Tapta, Bhayānaka, Kṣār, Viṭ, Mūtra, Śleṣma, Duḥsaha, Gara, Dūṣikā, Vasā, Śukra, Āsṛka, Aśru, Gātramala, Karna, Maviṭa, Mansa, Nakra, Loma, Keśa, Ashti, Tāmra, Kleśaprada, Mahān Pratapta Loha, Carma, Taptasurā, Tīkṣṇakanṭaka, Viṣavistāraka, Viś, Tailapratapta, Durbaha Kunta, Kṛmi, Pūya, Durantaka, Sarpa, Maśaka, Danśa, Bhayankar, Bhayankara, Garal, Śsara, Śula, Bhayankara Khadaga, Gola, Nakra (Ī) Kāla, Manthāna, Duhasaha Tapta Pāṣāṇa Tīkṣṇa Pāṣāṇa, Lālā, Masī, Cūrna, Cakra, Vakra,

Kūrma, Mahāna Asahya Jwālā, Bhasma, Dagdha, Taptasūcī, Asipatra, Kṣuradhāra, Sūcīmukha, Nakramukha, Gokāmukha, Gajadanśa, Gomukha and Kumbhīpāka, Kālasūtra, Matsyaoda, Kṛmi, Pānśubhojya, Paśaveṣṭa, Śūlaprota, Prakampana, Ulkāmukha, Andhakūpa, Vedhana and Tāṇḍana, Jwālārandhra, Dehachūraṇa, Dalana, Śoṣaṇaka, Śūrpajvālāmukha, Dhūmāndha and Nāgaveṣṭana.

Vaitarni Nadi

For the proper maintenance of the aforesaid ponds, one million attendants were appointed for ever. Holding plenty of staves and massive maces in their hands, they keep on working ceaselessly. Putting on the formidable and dreadful appearance, they are not subject to any control and command with the exception of Lord of Death. They are full of rage and fury in conformity with the nature of their action.

At the time of demise, they appear before sinners but not to those who worship gods and goddesses. In brief, the consequences of certain wrong actions following dealt, are given below.

The Fate of Bribery

Tax Defaulter

The Fate of a Butcher

The Fate of a Prostitute

The Fate of a False Speaker

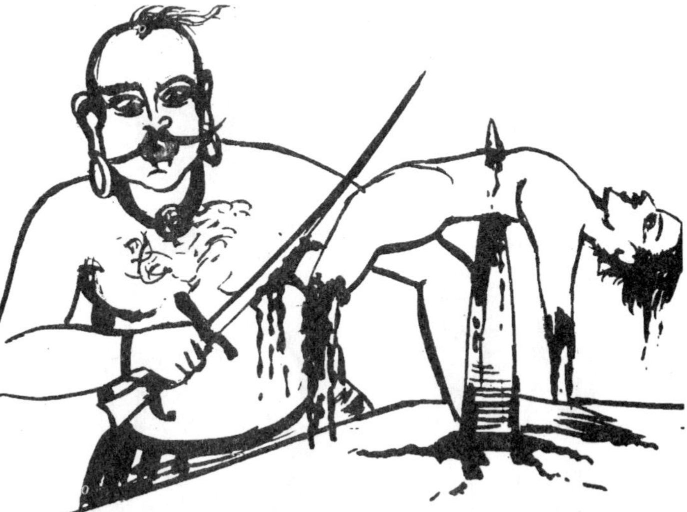

The Fate of a Black Marketeer

Over loader of Animals

The Fate of a Thief

A Brāhmin (a member of the highest Hindu priestly caste) who shares food with an adulteress or a harlot and accompanies her becomes a victim to Kālasūtra Kuṇḍ sometimes he becomes a partridge for seven births. Those who dine on the inauspicious occasion of the solar and the lunar eclipses, lead to Aruntuda Kuṇḍa. Despite the performance of the betrothal of their daughters, those who get them married to some others, are doomed to go to Pansakuṇḍa. Those who make a brāhmin speechless by virtue of wrong arguments are forced to join Prankampan. Those women who talk to their husbands in a tempestuously furious way, make their way to Ulkamukha. A prostitute is compelled to guide her steps to Vedhana. Those who are administered in false oath, go to Jwalamukha but those who falsely swear calling upon Śalagrama, are condemned to be born as the insects from excreta for seven times. Those who usurp the property of deities and Brāhmins force their way to Dhūmrandha.

DEITIES DWELLING IN THE HUMAN BODIES

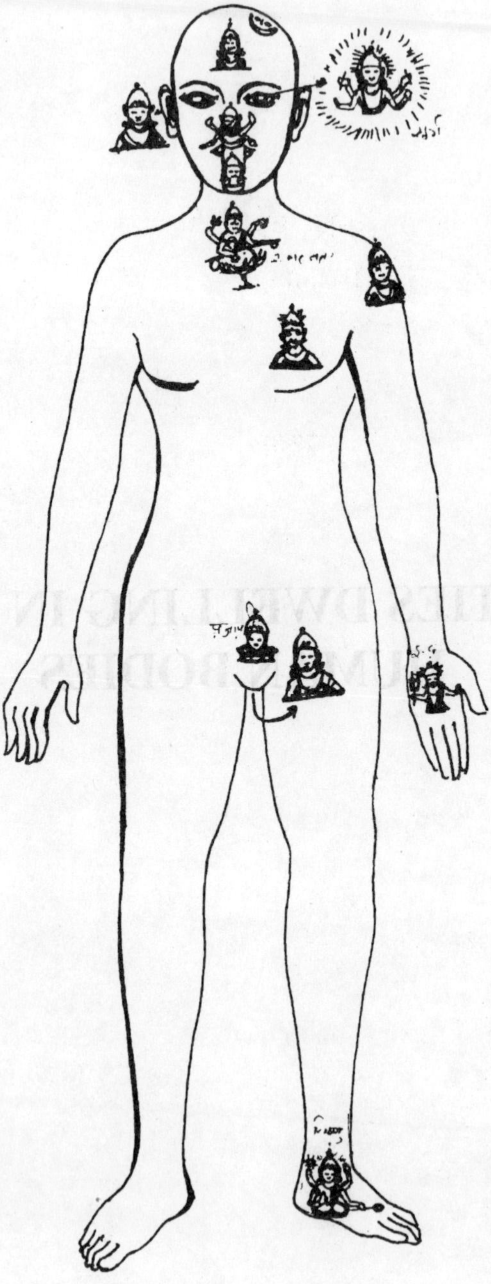

DEITIES DWELLING IN THE HUMAN BODIES

It would be very insightful and interesting to mention that the Omnipresent, Omniscient, Omnipotent and the Universal Soul having created the Universe, permeated through it and pervaded it. Hereafter, all the deities entered this elegant creation with Him. God made trees, aquatic animals, birds, insects, and moths, viz., various sorts of animate and inanimate things. On the contrary, it is also remarkable that He Himself was not with his own creation and then he was inclined to create the human body endowed with the sovereign-quality like rationality and discretionary power. This is the quality which distinguishes between man and animal throughout the world. Through this quality, man can commune with the Supreme Being in a very natural way.

There are three and a half crore nerves in this body and in the same proportion, there are deities herein. Almost all of them are found invisibly but fourteen of them are apparently perceptible.

1. The deity of the eyes, the organ of seeing-The Sun-god belongs to the eyes and he is the presiding deity of the eyes, organ of seeing. This is the reason that any form or colour is perceived through this sense-organ. Heliolatry is scientifically beneficial in human life.

2. The deity of olfactory senses (the nasal organ)—Aśvanī Kumār is the presiding deity of the nose. Through it, we have the pleasant or the unpleasant sensation of smell.

3. The deity of the organ of hearing-The Direction is the deity of the ear through which speech is heard.

4. The glossal deity—Neptune lies on the tip of the tongue which gives the taste of a thing.

5. The deity of the skin-God, the wind, lies all over the skin through which there is the sensation of touch.

6. The deity of the hands—Lord Indra belongs to the hands which play a major role to receive everything in the world.

7. The deity of the feet—Lord Viṣṇu, the most famous Vedic deity indwells the feet.

8. The deity of speech—Mother Sarasvatī is closely associated with speech viz. she is the presiding deity of speech.

9. The deity of the genital organs—These are the private parts of the human body. They are the fountain of delight and herein there is the abode of Prajāpati (the maintainer of subjects).

10. The deity of the Anus—Through this organ of the human body, the excretion of excrement or faces is possible. The deity known as Mitra abides in this part.

11. The Deity of the organ of intellect—Brahmā, the creator of the universe, is the governing deity of intellect through which each and every thing is known.

12. The Deity of Pride—Rudra (the eleven inferior manifestations of Lord Śiva) is the deity of pride.

13. The Deity of the Mind—The moon is the presiding deity of the mind. The concentration of mind is yoga (a union with the Universal Soul by means of contemplation).

14. The Deity of the heart—The heart is fraught with consciousness. The pulsation in any part of the body that is chiefly due to the heart. Even Saccidānanda consisting of three words sat, cita, and anand (the Supreme Being, the personification of three attributes-truth, consciousness and bliss) flows to the universe only from the heart which inspirits each and every iota of the entire universe. The force of nature is its deity. God always abides in the mind. Only through the practice of religious devotion, God fulfils one's desires. The human body contains the six plexuses wherein all gods as well as goddesses abide.

A man having good mental and physical health sound mind and sound body inhales and exhales 21,600 times round the clock. Mantras or hymns like Hansah, Soham continue to the chanted effortlessly. It is called Ajapa-Japa. (Japa-the repetition of the name of a deity).

Pelvic Plexus (Mūlādhāra Cakra)	The great God, Gaṇapati, gifted with accomplishments and intellect belongs to the pelvic plexus.
Hypogastric Plexus (Svādhisṭhāna Cakra)	Brahmā the creator of the universe, remains with his consort Sarasvatī inside the Hypogastric Plexus,
Epigastric Plexus or the Solar Plexus (Manīpura Cakra)	Viṣṇu, in the company of his consort Lakṣmī, belongs to the Epigastric Plexus.
Cardiac Plexus (Anāhat Cakra)	Lord Śiva in the company of Goddess Pārvatī belongs to this plexus.
Carotid Plexus (Viśuddha Cakra)	The individual soul with the vital force refers to the carotid Plexus.
Medula Plexus (Ājñā Cakra)	The preceptor (Gurū) endowed with the power of knowledge remains inside the Medula Plexus. He is also reputed to be the organ of clairvoyance.
Cerebral Plexus (Sahastrāra Cakra)	Because of having close association with Lord Śiva, ambrosia streams from the mind.

The body is a temple and several deities belong to it in the company of the individual soul.

Note. For a detailed study of the six plexuses please refer to page number... in the Goddess section of this book.

ARDHANĀRĪŚVARA

Lord Śiva assumes multi forms: Arddhanārīśvara is the best one. The literal meaning of the word 'Arddhanārīśvara' is the combination of two different forms—male and female. The form of Arddhanārīśvara is to be pondered over for the sake of clarity in two ways; internal and external. As we know that the discipline of science which observes experiments and analyses a concrete thing is confined to the circumference of a circle having a particular centre. It points out that without contra position, there will be no creation, viz. just as plus and minus being contradictory joins two even or odd numbers in the same way male and female combine and They manifest in the multifarious, multicoloured and multidimensional creation. It is extraordinarily divine in appearance. On the surface, although it sounds strange to the human eyes after a minute observation and profound meditation, the real image of God emerges. This is inexplicable as it is abstract. True, this benign form consists of a great ideal of human race. This can be illustrated by a fine example of a singularly graceful image of this deity located at the cave of Elora in Maharastra. This idol is identified as that of Arddhanārīśvara. It goes without saying that the iconographer had spiritual sense to the background of this structure.

The SUPREME BEING consists of three forms—*Sat, Cit and Ānand* (the purest Being, the purest essence of consciousness and the purest essence of Bliss eternal). Śiva is considered to be all pervading Ānand which is the goal of human beings. Though the three attributes belong to man's mind but

due to ignorance he or she is not able to commune with the Ultimate Reality. The truth is that when Sat and Cit combine, we realise and identify ourselves with God.

The appearance of the purest being of God is regarded as maternal one and this appearance of the purest essence of consciousness is paternal one. It is his third appearance which denotes the purest essence of Bliss eternal wherein paternity harmonizes with maternity, to wit, Śiva and Śakti combine together and emerge as Arddhanārīśvara. He is also called Yogiśvara but indeed he is the god of householders. He is worthy of worshipful adoration in the eyes of a married couple. The fact is that he is the manifestation of the consummate union of male and female.

From the external standpoint, his family is an ideally and unusually living model of diversity. The members of Lord Śiva's family have different ways and views. Śiva mounts on a bull and his consort, Bhagawatī is seated on a lion. He has two sons: Kārtikeya and Gaṇeśa. The former likes a peacock as his vehicle and the latter has fondness for a mouse as a vehicle. One moves slowly and the other moves fast.

Śiva's head is always graced with the Ganges and it is believed to be the cause of extreme jealousy between co-wives. In this way, fuss or imbroglio continues to cloud his household, like a pannier fraught with different sorts of things. The appearance of Arddhanārīśvara conveys to us a message that one should always be happy even after being confronted and beset with a lot of incoherence and contradictions. This appearance endows one with artha, dharma, kāma, mokṣa (wealth religion, sex and liberation). At last it can be said that one who leads even the life of a household, can realise Arddhanārīśvara Śiva, the embodiment of the purest essence of Bliss eternal.

Note: The symbolic significance of various forms, shapes and things possessed by Lord Śiva can be seen in the chapter on Lord Śiva. Further the other half of Arddhanārīśvara (the female shape) represented by Durgā can be located on the appropriate chapter devoted to Durgā.

NAVA DURGĀS
(NINE GODDESSES)

NAVA DURGĀS

The great and merciful goddess *Durgā* bears nine impor tant and sublime forms. All of them represent the mysteries of the spiritual world. First of all there arises a question, "Why are there only Nava Durgās? A direct and logical answer to this question is given below:

Mathematically or statistically, 'nine' is considered to be the largest digit numerically. On the contrary, on the basis of the *Vedas* and other Hindu religious scriptures, we come to know that 'nine' is symbolically a 'Supreme Power'. It is universal, undivided, wonderful and unalterable.

For example:

9X1 =09;	9X2 = 18	1+8 =9
9X3 =27	2+7 = 9	
9X5 =45	4+5 = 9	

The *Vedas* and other scriptures are said to have pointed out the exact number of days, i.e., 360 days in one year. According to Astrology, one moon month consists of 360 days. In Geometry, a circle is drawn at 360°. In Geography, there is only one circle, therefore, it is called zero.

Divide 360 by 9 and the answer will be 40.

A considerable amount of importance is attached to this figure in *Tantra*.

In the transcendental or spiritual world, there is one zero of 40 days.

Four types of *Nava-Rātris* have been mentioned in the Vedas:

1. *Caitra* (March and April)
2. *Āśvina* (September and October)
3. *Pūṣa* (December and January)
4. *Āṣāḍha* (June and July)

But normally the overwhelming majority of devotees repose their unflinching faith in the two of these months. During the *Nava-Rātri,* each of the goddesses is offered prayers on a particular night in order to exterminate evils and preserve truth and religion. The nine forms of *Durgās* are detailed in the different and classic chapters.

THE NINE GODDESSES

ŚAILAPUTRĪ

Śailaputrī is one who is worshipped on the first night of Navarātra. This is the first form of goddess Durgā. She is reputed to be Śailaputrī because she is the first and the elder daughter of king Śaila (Himālaya or Himavāna). She is ceremoniously and traditionally worshipped by a large number of devotees. The sādhakas (practitioners of Kuṇḍalinī Yoga) worship the goddess on the first night in order that they may closely associate himself with the plexus of Kuṇḍalinī yoga. The deity is referred to the cakra (plexus). Her vehicle is said to be a bull. Her two hands represent twin sorts of power—Śiva and Nature, small and great, corporeal and incorporeal. Her left hand has a lotus-flower which marks plasticity, sweetness, welfare, benevolence and energy. A trident suits one of her hands, in the likewise manner in the Greek mythology, Neptune has been shown carrying a weapon like a trident. The goddess holds this weapon to annihilate monsters, demons and wrong doers i.e. it is designed for the provision for punishment. This weapon also symbolises the triumph of good over evil. She bears the world-illumining moon on her head. The moon stands for beauty, happiness. The goddess looks like the rising sun.

BRAHMACĀRIṆĪ

On analysis, the world 'Brahmacāriṇī' consists of two words—'Brahma' and 'Cāriṇī'. These words are derived from the Saṁskṛta language. 'Brahma' stands for the Supreme Being and 'Cāriṇī' for a follower i.e. seeker of the Ultimate Reality. She is the second incarnation of the great goddess Durgā. She is always found engrossed and steeped in the prayer and worship of the formless God. The form of the goddess denotes illumination, divinity and auspiciousness. Her countenance is bright and radiant. She is white complexioned. She is gifted with all the extraordinary qualities but she never dissociates herself from the Bliss (Brahma). She has two hands. She possesses a very nice vase containing nectar for the welfare of mankind in one hand. In the next, there is a rosary by means of which she invokes and worships Brahma. This rosary epitomises single mindedness.

This day a devotee offers worshipful devotion to Brahmacāriṇī in order that he may rivet his attention on Svādhisthāna Cakra (Hypogastric Plexus) and also ensure his accomplishments and achievements.

CANDRAGHAṆṬĀ

This is the third and sweetly graceful appearance of the great and benign goddess Durgā known as Candraghaṇṭā. This name consists of two words—Candra stands for the moon and Ghaṇṭā for a bell. She bears a lunar shape on her head like a bell; therefore, she is called Cahndraghaṇṭā. With a great amount of luminosity, she is gold complexioned in her appearance. The lion is considered to be gorgeous vehicle of the goddess. She is ten handed. They represent the ten directions of the world, ten organs of the body—five sense organs and five action organs. The waves of the welcome and resonant sound emanate from her divine appearance. The lion symbolises boldness and courage. A large number of devoices worship her and concentrate on 'Maṇipur Cakra' (the epigastric or solar plexus for the sake of accomplishments or Siddhis).

KŪṢMĀṆḌĀ

This is the fourth form of goddess Durgā who played a vital role in the complex and complicated process of the creation, which seems structurally beautiful, attractive and multicoloured. According to the śāstra (scripture), before the creation, there was nothing but darkness all around i.e., the whole universe was plunged into darkness. It came into existence by means of a wonderfully extreme and sanguine laughter caused by Kūṣmāṇḍā. She incarnated herself for this purpose so she is the primal form of goddess. She is gifted with an unlimited amount of energy i.e., her laughter was energy. She belongs to the Solar System from which an excessive amount of warmth and heat continues to emanate. The heat provides energy to all the living and non-living objects. Many worshippers appear before the image of the goddess to worship her. Practitioners squat in front of her to meditate and concentrate upon the Cardiac Plexus (Anāhat Cakra) to facilitate accomplishments. She is the deity of Anāhat Cakra. She possesses eight arms representing eight Bhairavas, eight accomplishments. She has a particular sort of vase containing divine water symbolising life. Thus every creature gets a lease of life from her. She brings up and looks after them whilst simultaneously annihilating the creation i.e., everything is subservient to her power. She has a divine wheel signifying motion or life thus conveying a universal message to achieve the goal of life by walking along the path of action incessantly. A bow and arrow adorn her hands standing for female and male respectively.

SKANDAMĀTĀ

'Skandamātā is said to be the fifth form of the great goddess Durgā. She is the mother of Skanda who is shown getting seated on her lap. He is also called by another name Kārikeya. She is white complexioned in her appearance which represents simplicity, honesty and success. She possesses the three eyes which stand for Brahmā, Viṣṇu and Maheśa, the three worlds and also the sun, the moon and fire. She has four arms, which symbolises man's objective—dharma, artha, kāma and mokṣa (religion, wealth, sex and salvation). She holds two lotuses in her two hands. These flowers represent the sun and the moon which always guide all the creatures of the universe. The other two hands show boon-granting and protective postures. The lion which plays the role of a vehicle signifies dauntlessness, valiance and valour.

On the fifth day of '*Nava-Rātri*', millions of devotees offer their prayers to the goddess. At the same time practitioners and worshippers place themselves inside '*Viśuddha Cakra*' of '*Kuṇḍalinī Yoga*' by meditation.

KĀTYĀYANĪ

Kātyāyanī' is highly reputed to be the sixth form of the great goddess '*Durgā*'. She is the daughter of sage '*Kātya*'. This is the reason that she is called 'Kātyāyanī'. She is of gold complexion in her sublime appearance. She is the presiding deity of Vrajamaṇḍala. She possesses four arms which hold four different objects. In one hand, she has a sword which represents wisdom, enlightenment, a device to dispel ignorance and good fortune. The second hand is graced with a lotus flower which signifies beauty and magnificence from the physical point of view but from the spiritual standpoint, it stands for Brahma. The other two hands symbolise fearlessness and boon-granting poses. All four arms also display the four eras and the four '*Vedas*'. She has three eyes which epitomise physical, moral and spiritual standpoints. A red mark on her forehead marks beauty and good fortune. She mounts on the lion which is the symbol of courage and boldness.

On the sixth day, a practitioner or devotee concentrates on the Medula Plexus. According to religious scriptures, a spinster offers prayers to the goddess in order to be blessed with an obedient, handsome, and polite life partner.

KĀLARĀTRĪ (Śītalā)

The seventh form of goddess Durgā is said to be that of *Kālarātri*. She is of black and dark complexion. Her hair is flowing and unkempt. She has four arms. The two hands of the right side represent blessing and fearless poses. The next two of the left side are fitted with a cleaver and thunder-bolt. The former signifies wisdom, enlightenment and good fortune. The latter stands for the extermination of the various kinds of ignorance. She is blessed with the three eyes which represent the three important things such as the sun, the moon and fire. She has a wondrous kind of chain round her neck. It is bright and lucent like electric light. She mounts on a donkey, called *gadahā* which is derived from the Saṁskṛt language. *Gadaha* signifies a physician. After the separation of the constituents in the conjunct word *'gadahā'* we have the following:

Gada+Hā

'Gad' means ailment and *'Hā'* means reliever (one who relieves someone of any sort of disease or malady). In this way, by the instrumentality of this creature, she communicates to us that it is not an ordinary type of creature but it is an embodiment of a physician. The symbolic meaning of the donkey is diligence and self-contentment which should be possessed by the entire humanity. It is also propounded in Āyurveda

and when the dried excreta of the donkey is burnt, the smoke thus produced relieves a patient of small-pox and chicken-pox.

Externally she appears to have formidable and hopelessly dangerous appearance but internally she is full of generosity, motherliness, politeness, compassion and commiseration.

MAHĀGAURĪ

Mahāgaurī is reputed to be eighth form of the great goddess '*Durgā*'. *Mahāgaurī = Mahā+Gaurī*. Mahā means great and Gauri means white colour. She is purely fair complexioned. The complexion of her appearance is put in comparison with the moon which illumines the entire world with its silvery and soothing beams. She is compared even to a conch-shell and a particular flower named *Kund*. She always remains eight years old. Her age stands for the eight sorts of accomplishments (*Siddhis*). Her wearing apparel as well as ornaments are also white. The white complexion marks simplicity, truth, purity, peace and sattvaguṇa. She has four arms. In one hand, she holds a trident which represents the best device to relieve mankind of three kinds of sorrows. Her other two hands denote blessing and protective poses. She has a kind of drum or tabor which dispels the darkness and ignorance of the human kind. She mounts on a bull that symbolises dharma (religion). Her original name was '*Pārvatī*' who did penance to please and propitiate *Lord Śiva* to get married. This penance blackened her appearance. On the contrary, it gladdened and delighted him. As a result, he fully washed her body with the consecrated water of the *Gangā*. Since the very day, she had come to be known as *Mahāgaurī*.

She has two earrings in her two ears which signify the two attributes of nature—the first is *rajas* and the second *tamas*.

The divine appearance of the goddess refers to *sat*. All these attributes contribute to the creation of the universe. On the eighth day of *Nava-Rātri*, millions of devotees worship her in order to cherish worldly and spiritual bliss.

SIDDHIDĀTRĪ

This is the ninth form of the charmingly divine appearance which the great goddess Durgā bears. She is known as Siddhidātrī because she grants her devotees various types of boons and accomplishments. She is shown seated on a lotus-flower which represents deliverance. She has four arms. In one of her hands, she had held a lotus-flower which stands for the Indestructible, Omnipotent, Omnipresent and Omniscient Ultimate Reality. The Second hand is graced with a wheel which marks sixteen kinds of sacraments as well as the same number of ritual performances and progress. In the third hand, she has a conch-shell which characterises the inception of the creation, infinite space, germicide, *satoguṇa* and knowledge. In her fourth hand she has a mace which stands for the power of constant law of nature. Its top round part signifies a skull; its shaft shows the spinal chord and primal learning (Ādividyā). A radiant chain round her neck marks unity which is the need and requirement of the hour for the good and welfare of humanity. Remarkably enough, only by the grace of the goddess, Śiva could assume an incomparably graceful appearance which came to be known as Arddhanārīśvara throughout the world.

TANTRIK GODDESSES

DAŚA MAHAVIDYĀ
(THE TEN GREAT TEACHINGS)

DAŚA MAHAVIDYĀ
(THE TEN GREAT TEACHINGS)

The ten great teachings (Dasamahāvidyā) comprise an im portant galaxy of female deities. They are reputed to be the respectful and graceful manifestations of the Ultimate Reality. They are worshipped by Brahmā, Viṣṇu and Maheśa. All these gods are active and energetic only by the grace of the goddesses; Brahmā is able to hold the responsibility of creation. Viṣṇu is capable of nursing, bringing up and observing animate and inanimate objects existing in the entire cosmos. In the concluding state, Lord Śiva also derives energy and power from Mahāvidyās to annihilate the whole creation.

The Signification and Significance of 'Ten'

There was a time when the universe was 'non-existent'. Zero was the point. But the point was not zero which stands for consummate. Astrology is also in support of it. Noticeably the figures like 1, 2, 3, 4, 5, 6, 7, 8, and 9, gradually evolved out of the point. In other words, all the figures concluded on 09. After the end of 9, figure 01, was alotted with zero (01 is followed by zero) and it was termed as 'ten'. The figure marks the ten directions of the world and the ten organs of the human body.

From the transcendental standpoint (the Supreme Being) and Mahāvidyā are inseparable and identical. There arises a question, "Why is Śaktitattva (the Supreme Goddess) termed as Vidyā or Mahāvidyā?" The appropriate and logical answer to this question counts on spiritual knowledge with regard to the glowing and radiant appearance of the trinity of Realities. He being blessed with wealth, knowledge, special element and astounding activities, is regarded as Akṣar Brahma (indestructible Ultimate Reality).

The following descriptions regarding each of the forms of the goddess are presented in different chapters.

KĀLĪ

Amid ten sorts of great teachings '*Mahāvidyās*', '*Kālī*' holds the first and most valuable position. The word '*Kālī*' literally signifies black or dark complexion. It is the benign goddess '*Kālī*' whose countenance is of black complexion. In her appearance she is very awful and dreadful. She is in the state of nature and standing posture. She lives in the cremation-ground. She assumes various forms but here she has incarnated herself assuming ten forms of the goddess according to the need of hour. Some of her forms are very fierce but some of them are fairly graceful.

Remarkably, the space between the earth and the sky is considered to be '*Kālī*'. She appeared from '*Mahāmāyā*' (the Supreme Goddess) She is said to be the principal deity of '*tantra-sādhanā*'. Her hand is armed with a severed head.

She possesses four arms. The two represent blessing and fearless poses. The third holds a blood stained or bloodied cleaver which stands for wisdom and enlightenment. The fourth one is equipped with the human skull that symbolises the controller and retainer of the universe and truthfulness respectively. These four arms stand for the four '*Vedas*', the four eras, the four stages of life, a garland of decapitated heads is dangling round her neck. These heads symbolise the alphabet. The major portion of her tongue hangs out while the minor portion of that is pressed between the teeth. The tongue stands for 'Rajas'

and '*Tamas*' and the teeth for '*Sattva*'. She has long disheveled hair which stands for diversity. She wears a girdle of several arms round her waist.

TĀRĀ

The term 'Tārā' is derived from the root word of Sanskrit '*Taran*' which stands for the deliverance of mankind from the bondage of birth and death. She is seen standing on a corpse and puts on a tiger skin. The bright rays are emanating from her three mystical eyes. She has dishevelled trees that a yellowish. She wears a garland of decapitated heads and she possesses four arm; in all of her hands, she hold four types of items such as scissors, a lotus, a cleaver and a begging skull.

Significantly, it is said that there exist fifty zeroes in the midst of the cosmos. Five of them are under the governance and influence of Tārā, who bears a festive and blue complexioned appearance which is the symbol of the unknown blue sky. In order to ward off mankind from disasters and calamities, she assumes a fierce and formidable appearance. Her four arms symbolise *Dharma*, *Artha*, *Kāma*, *Mokṣa*. Ṭhe scissors are expressively the symbolic representation of a marvellous device which extirpates the evil ideas leading to illusion and worldly affairs. The dual parts of the scissors stand for the two aspects of life: the first is salacious life and the second is deliverance. The begging skull (*Khappar*) represents integral life. The corpse marks the ephemeral world. Her lustrous head is like the sun and her trees the countless stars.

CHINNAMASTĀ

'*Chinnamastā*' holds the third position amid ten great teachings (*Daśamahāvidyās*). Kabandha is the presiding deity of the swiftly changing world. Her appearance is enveloped in mystery. She is profoundly introverted so her devotee strains every nerve to go into the depth of mystery. The state of her being introvert indicates that she is always absorbed in profound meditation. She has two arms which represent heaven and hell, weal and woe, good and evil, virtues and vices, merits and demerits. She is the embodiment of truth. She stands in the cremation-ground on the bodies of '*Kāma*' (sex) and *Rati* (passion). She has beheaded herself with the sword that is held by her in one of her hands. In the next, she possesses a platter. The three streams or jets of blood spurt from her neck and flow into the mouths of the twin female assistants. These three jets stand for '*sattvaguṇa*, '*rajogṇa*' and '*tamoguṇa*'. They also stand for '*Brahmā*', '*Viṣṇu*' and '*Śiva*' and again cough, bile and wind. One jet of blood flows into the goddess's mouth and the remaining jets of blood into the mouths of her both attendants who mark '*rajoguṇa*' and '*tamoguṇa*'. She quenches their thirst with her own blood. In this way it is crystal clear that her incarnation is aimed at the welfare of a host of devotees.

According to yogaśāstra, there are three glands—'*Brahmā*', '*Viṣṇu*' and '*Rudra*' which are located respectively in '*Mūlādhāra*' *Cakra* (Pelvic plexus), '*Maṇipura Cakra*' (Epigastric plexus), and '*Ājñā Cakra*' (Medula plexus). These three jets of blood spurt from the goddess's neck signify the three glands. After concentrating on and having close connection with these glands a devotee realises and communes with the goddess.

ṢOḌAṢĪ

'*Ṣoḍaṣī*' is the name of the noble minded and merciful and goddess who holds the fourth position among the highly esteemed ten great teachings. She stands out just like the glowing and glorious sun which is ornamented with the gold complexion at the break of day. She is sixteen years old and she is found squatting in the middle of an attractive lotus on the prostrate body of '*Lord Śiva*'. Both of them are on a base supported by the trinity of the great gods '*Brahmā*', '*Rudra*', '*Viṣṇu*' and '*Indra*'. She possesses four arms and three eyes. She holds in her hands various sort of defensive devices such as a chain, a hook, a bow and an arrow. Remarkably, Śiva is the power-house of force and energy which the goddess incessantly derives in order to rotate the wheel of time.

According to the facts propounded by the science of '*Tantra*', she has five faces which are those of '*Lord Śiva*'. The colour of the faces is red, blue, smoky, green and yellow. She is proficient in sixteen traditional types of make-up so she is called '*Ṣoḍaṣī*'. Her four arms symbolise '*Brahmā*', '*Viṣṇu*', '*Rudra*' and '*Yama*'. She possesses a strong noose which stands for attraction. By means of the noose, she commands and controls the world. She has five arrows that mark the five elements out of which the entire creation and the physical body are composed. There is a hook in her hand which is the symbol of 'restraint upon desire' and salvation. The lotus-flower

which emanates from the small navel in the middle of the surface of the belly of '*Lord Shiva*', represents welfare. The wreath of hers signifies unity and integrity. She blesses one indulgence in luxury and salvation.

BHUVANEŚVARĪ

It is Bhuvaneśvarī who is the goddess of glory and lustre. She holds the fifth position amid ten great teachings (*Mahāvidyās*). She nourishes and nurtures the three worlds, so she is reputed to be Bhuvaneśvarī. According to *Devī Purāṇa*, another name of primal or cardinal nature is Bhuvaneśvarī. Even the left part of Lord Śiva is said to be Bhuvaneśvarī. She plays a vital role in the cosmic play performed by him. She is as delicate as silk. She looks like the reddish glow of the dawn in her festive appearance. She smiles pleasantly. She has four arms: in two of them, she holds a hook or goad and a noose which are the main weapons which stand for respectively restraint and attachment. The next two hands show blessing and protective poses. Her head is graced with the crown of the moon.

She is gifted with the three lustrous eyes which represent *sattva, rajas and tamas* and also *Brahmā, Viṣṇu* and *Maheśa.* From these eyes the stream of water constantly gushes and quenches the thirst of all the creatures of the mortal world. All the rivers and seas also rise in them. She has enormous breasts that always ooze the required amount of milk for all the creatures. She also feeds those who belong to this creation. This is the reason that she is called Śakambharī.

TRIPURABHAIRAVĪ

Kālabhairo is the abode of this mortal and ephemeral world as well as the great goddess. Tripura is his energy and power. She holds an important position amid ten great teachings (*Mahāvidyās*). She has ruddy and robust personality. The colour of her body is red. She is clothed in red. She wears a wreath of severed skulls that stand for the alphabet. Her bosom is smeared with blood which epitomizes the menstrual fluid of the process of the creation. She has four arms: in the first, she holds a garland which stands for single-mindedness and the perpetual cycle of time. In the second, she has a book which marks valuable learning and knowledge of *Brahma*. The third and the fourth show the explicit expressions of protection and benediction or boon. She is graced with the three eyes that are the symbols of the three Vedas—*Ṛg*, *Yajur* and *Sām*. From sixteen letters of alphabet are Bhairo and 'K' to 'Kṣa' i.e., thirty three consonantal letters of alphabet *Bhairavī*. She is known as *Kālrātri* as she is referred to the night. At the same time *Bhairo* is said to be *Kāla Bhairo*.

According to *Āgam* Scriptures, She is reputed to be Om, the Almighty. She is also the presiding deity of the primal cause of minute speech and the creation. In order to have rigorous restraint upon desires, sense and action organs, a constellation of saints, sages, devotees and practitioners worship the goddess who assumes various forms for the good and benevolence of all the creatures of the entire creation.

DHŪMĀVATĪ

Dhūmāvatī holds the seventh position amidst the *Daś Mahāvidyās*. She herself is the great female energy and controller of the world. Since her life-partner or husband is no more, she is called a widow. Her popularly known name is Dhūmra or Dhūmāvatī as she had already caused *Lord Śiva* to go down the throat driven by extreme hunger and thirst and hereafter the fumes started emanating from her body. She is of dusky and tenebrious complexion. She is of long stature, fidgety. She is shabbily and poorly dressed. Her hair is dishevelled. She possesses large and pendulous breasts. Her nose is long and crooked. She is pugnacious and quick-tempered. She rides a chariot equipped with a flag on which there sits a crow. She has a winnowing basket in one hand which is the symbol of the abnegation of worthless things; she is also the symbol of the affirmation of permanent and valuable things of the universe. The dark colour of the crow symbolises the mind indulged in lust and attachment. On the contrary, positively a single eye of the crow represents single mindedness or the concentration of mind.

There are three kinds of sorrows-bodily, worldly and godly. These are caused by the four deities: fever, mania, burning sensation by *Rudra*; faint, disablement, by *Yama*; gout, paralysis by Neptune; grief, troubles driven by hunger, thirst, etc., by *Nirriti* that is another name of Dhūmāvatī.

VAGALĀMUKHĪ

Vagalāmukhī is the deity of glory and lustre and occupies the eighth position in the midst of *Daśa Mahāvidyās* (ten great teachings). Valgā mentioned in *Nigama Śāstra* (Deductive Science) is *Bagalāmukhī* in *Āgama Śāstra* (Inductive Science). She ascends the gemmed throne under a canopy carved out of jewels. Yellow ornaments, a garland and clothes add to the beauty of her lovely appearance.

From the individualistic standpoint, her energy is aimed at destroying foes, on the other hand, from the collectivistic point of view, annihilating the entire creation. She is a two handed goddess: in the first, she holds a mace with which she smashes her foes and with the second she draws out their tongues. A mace symbolises nose and the tongue, the manifestation of the entire creation out of pitch darkness. This is an important part of the human body and also the means of expression of thoughts and feelings. She is being and becoming both. It is interesting to mention that *Atharvā* is a particular element that normally continues to be expressed from within body. It is not in a concrete form so it is not perceptible. It is a type of wireless telegraphy. Practically, our mind is overwhelmed with an invisible power. The same is called *Atharvā* by means of which a man can be summoned from a very large distance. It is one of the best detectors.

She is generally worshipped in Order to be free from the dread and fear of foes and to be blessed with the power of speech.

MĀTAṄGĪ

Mātaṅgī holds the ninth position in the midst of the *Daśa Mahāvidyās.* 'Mātaṅgī' means the greatest amount of power which is said to have been derived from '*Mātaṅga*', that is the synonym for '*Lord Śiva*'. The appearance of the great goddess is very attractive and glorious in black and blue complexion. Her head is crowned with the ever shining moon. She has three eyes which roll in intoxication. She is seated on the gemmed throne and she is lustrous like a blue lotus-flower. She has also been compared to a forest conflagration which is capable of reducing to ashes a number of giants like a forest. She has four arms which are adorned with a noose, a goad, a shield and a cleaver. The charm of all these things holds the giants spell bound; on the other hand, the same things fulfill the cherished desires or the objectives of a host of devotees.

Her three eyes epitomise the sun, the moon and fire. Her four arms represent the four Vedas. The noose stands for a godly efficacy to entrap ignorance, control over desires, a goad for restraint upon desire, liberation from Avidyā (ignorance). The attributes of sense-organs such as sight, hearing, smell, taste and touch fall under the sword which signifies for the five primary elements of the creation–water, earth, air, fire and ether. By the side of the goddess, a parrot is seen chanting something that stands Hṛṇ i.e. *bijāṅkūr* (seed). She puts one of her legs on a lotus-flower which signifies the creation of letters. Her body appears to be tinged with honey which is like ambrosia, and her blood-coloured dress represents fire, knowledge and victory. To *Tāntrikas*, she is *Mātaṅgī* and to *Vaidiks*, she is *Sarasvatī* (Goddess of learning).

KAMALĀ

Kamalā holds the tenth position in the midst of *Daś Mahāvidyās*. Remarkably, the word 'Kamalā' directly refers to 'Kamala' (lotus-flower) which grows in the mire of water. Since she has appeared from Adam's ale, so it is tenable to address her Kamalā. With a view to the attainment of nectar, the churning of the fathomless sea by a host of gods and demons resulted in the graceful appearance of the great goddess Kamalā who chose *Lord Viṣṇu* to be her spouse. So she is said to be the energy of the spouse with whom she plays a vital role in a cosmic play. She is called by various names such as *Lakṣmī*, *Ṣoḍaṣī*, *Tripur*ā and *Bhārgavī*.

She is characterised as an exotic, radiant and lady of gold complexion. She is surrounded by many white elephants. They pour pitchers of fresh water over her. She ascends the throne of a lotus-flower. She is beautifully clothed in silk. She has four arms: in two of her hands, she has the same type of flowers. The other two hands symbolise a charitable and protective posture and her head is crowned with a gemmed crown. Her close relation with the elephants signifies her royal position; their foreheads (elephants) stand for seriousness and wisdom; the four big pitchers represent the four *Vedas* pouring from the pitchers; her sitting pose shows her profound meditation. She is the presiding deity of physical property. She has an affinity

to the merciful goddess *Lakṣmī* who is blessed with truth, consciousness and bliss (*Saccidānanda*). She is worshipped by deities, men and also by demons.

FEMALE DEITIES

GĀYATRĪ

Since the time immemorial, the concept of deification has been in fashion in India. '*Gāyatrī*' is one of such instance in the Vedic scripture. Indeed '*Gāyatrī*' is a *Vedic* metre which has been deified and propounded by our ancient scholars and saints. Now she is universally acknowledged and recognised as a goddess, the potent power of powers. She is the mother of the '*Vedas*' and the destroyer of all evils, vices and sins. She removes all hurdles and obstacles. She is said to be the primal cause of everything and the fountain of divine wisdom. Everything in the universe—manifested or unseen—is the manifestation of '*Gāyatrī*' who is the repository of knowledge and science. She manifested three attributes—sattva (poise), rajas (desire) and tamas (stupor). The qualities with the pure consciousness assumes the three different forms and names—'*Brahmā*', '*Viṣṇu*' and '*Maheśa*' (creator, observer and destroyer respectively) who were once cast by *Gāyatrī* into the cradle of void, which was dangling by means of the chains of the four Vedas representing knowledge and enlightenment. She has three forms—*Saraswatī*, '*Lakṣmī*' and 'Kālī' because of having their different outstanding qualities, Sattva, rajas and tamas. According to '*Gāyatrī Saṁhitā*', she is the essence of all scriptures and sciences. No doubt, it is she who manifested all the Vedas. She has five faces that symbolise five kinds of vital air—'*Vyāna*' (excretory), '*Apāna*' (evacuatory), '*Samān*' (that which ensures distribution) '*Prāṇa*'(respiration) and '*Udāna*' (transforming energy); ether, water, fire, air and either (the five elementary elements of the physical word), Pañcāmṛta, a sacred drink consisting of milk, yoghurt, sugar, clarified butter (ghee) and honey, '*Pañcāgni*', the five fires amidst which penance is performed as well as five sense-organs. She is clothed in red. Her appearance is put in comparison with the captivating full moon. She is gracefully seated on a lotus-flower. She is garlanded and graced with the numerous sorts of lustrous ornaments. She has ten arms holding some of celestial weapons—a club, a conch shell, lotus, boon-giving posture, fearless or protective pose, a goad, a skull, a wheel and a rosary. She is also graced with bracelets, ankle-bells and toe rings and gems. The arms stand for the ten directions and ten human organs, the five sense organs—eye, ear, nose, tongue and skin—and the five action organs—hand, feet, larynx, anus and genital organs.

The adoration and worship of the great Mother '*Gāyatrī*', is a road to achieve prosperity and progress not only from the phenomenal standpoint but also from the spiritual one.

Aum stands for Brahma (Ultimate Reality)

Aum Bhuvaḥ—God the creator

Aum Svaḥ—God, the Independent

Aum Tat—That perpetual God

Savitur—The dynamic and energetic tenet of light express ing through the sun

Vareṇyaṁ—The Ultimate Reality propitiated by a host of the greatest celestials

Bhargo—the greatest amount of effulgence blesses one with unspeakable joy, wisdom and knowledge.

Devasya—the light of the eternal God

Dhīmahi—we start profound meditation

Dhiyo—intellect

Yo—who/which

Naḥ—our

Pracodayāta—take to the fountain of light.

DURGĀ

The benign Goddess Durgā is the Supreme Power of the multi-dimensional cosmos. At the beginning, the creation emanates from her lustrous appearance and at the end gets dissolved in her. She assumes various forms having recourse to *Māyāśakti* (the mystical power) but, she is known as *Sākāra* and *Nirākāra* (formal and formless power). These are the two aspects of the same Reality. When *Māyāśakti* is in dynamic and active position, the great power supporting the 'Power of Illusion' is called 'A Formal Goddess' but when one is dissolved in the other, the Power of mystery turns *Nirguṇa*. There is a marked co-ordination between the two controversial qualities in her divine appearance. She is said to be the great creator, observer and annihilator as *Brahmā*, *Viṣṇu* and *Maheśa* have emerged from the fountain–head of her appearance. She being the fulcrum of Prakṛti (illusion) is the goddess of *Māyā*.

There is a clear inclusion of dualism and non-dualism here. She is *Pañcaśakti*, *Daśamahāvidyā*, *Navadurgā*, *Annapūrṇā*, *Kātyāyanī* and *Lalitāmbā*. She is not only a male energy but also a female energy. She is power and powerful both. She is shown as *Prakṛti*. The term '*Prakṛti*' stands for 'Pra+Kṛ+Ti' (as we know that all objectivity apart from the pure absolute subject consists of three aspects or guṇās). 'Pra' stands for *Sattva*, purity, goodness contemplation; 'Kṛ' for *Rajas*, smartness, the state of being active; 'Ti' for *Tamas*, 'evil passion'.

She is popularly known as *Durgā*. The term '*Durgā*' is analysed this way

'Dur' is a Saṁskṛt prefix.
'Du' stands for destruction or decay
'R' for the remedy for ailment
'Ga' for absolution from sin

In this connection, it is to be noted that she had killed the monstrous demon '*Durgam*' so she was named *Durgā* after him.

Her sweetly graceful appearance is incomparably and marvellously beautiful and delightful. Though there is also an account of the goddess having one thousand arms, it is out of question in the limited space of the book to convey any string of information with respect to this appearance.

Here it is my sincere effort to give the clear picture of the goddess possessing eighteen arms which represent eighteen *purāṇas*, the human body comprising the soul, five sense organs and five action organs, the mind and the six flaws of the mind such as sex, rage, desire, arrogance, envy and infatuation.

She holds a lot of items in all of her hands; a conch-shell, a goad, a serpent, an arrow, a shield, a trident, a mace, a spear, a cleaver, a noose or lasso, a wheel, a *parśu* (a battle axe), a thunder-bolt, a wreath, a bell, a knife, a skull. A conch-shell stands for the inception of the creation, infinite space, *sattva*, germicide, enlightenment; A goad or a hook signifies divine guidance, restraint upon desire, liberation from ignorance (*Avidyā*), knowledge to distinguish between worldly and spiritual affairs; a serpent for auspicious, inauspicious, venoms, nectar; a bow for balance between method and wisdom; an arrow is considered to be male energy but a bow is a female energy. The former represents *puruṣa* (male), but the latter

prakṛti (Nature) again a bow stands for five sense-organs, death-wish and awareness and an arrow for power of love; a shield denotes immunity against disease, a defensive device against demonic power. A trident = tri + dent (tri stands for three, dent for prongs), the symbolic meaning of this device is creator, preserver, and annihilator. Even the Sanskrit word '*Triśūla*' denotes the three things inside the human body such as Tri+Śūla, Tri for three, Śula for sorrows, i.e. three types of sorrows, three types of diseases–cough, bile and wind, will power, knowledge and action, three types of attributes–*Sattva*, *Rajas* and *Tamas*, three states of mind–conscious, sub-conscious and unconscious. A shaft for the axis of the creation, the spinal chord, the primal learning (Ādividyā) and wisdom: A mace for a ritual artifact, power of constant law of nature and its top round part for the skull: A spear for the concentration of mind and the Ultimate Reality: A cleaver for wisdom and enlightenment which drive away the worldly attachment and ignorance: A noose or lasso for godly efficacy to dispel ignorance, control over desire, attachment for worldly affairs: A wheel for fickle–mindedness, progress and it consists of twelve spokes and nine navels representing respectively the twelve signs of Zodiac–Aries, Taurus, Gemini, Cancer, Leo, Virgo, Libra, Scorpio, Sagittarius, Capricorn, Aquarius, Pisces and also for the twelve months. *Paraśu* (a battle-axe) is designed to overcome darkness and ignorance, and also for the spiritual path. A thunderbolt (*Vajra*) stands for the state of being indomitable, and represents the extermination of ignorance. A rosary, *Japamālā* signifies concentration and single mindedness, the perpetual cycle of time. A bell for primal sound and also signifies conquest of good over evil, success and prosperity. A knife symbolises liberation from worldly bondage.

At last it would be interesting to point out that there are nine well-known forms of *Durgā*, i.e. they are *Śailaputrī*,

Brahmacāriṇī, *Candraghaṇṭā, Kūṣmāṇḍā*, *Skandamātā*, *Kātyāyanī*, *Kālarātrī*, *Mahāgaurī*, and *Siddhidātrī* who endow material wealth in this world and spiritual advancement in the other.

MAHĀKĀLĪ OR DAKṢIṆA KĀLĪ

Since time immemorial, Dakṣnia Kālī has been one of the most celebrated and important deity who blessed a constellation of the *Maharṣi* seers of yore, the sages of whom the past, present and future were as an open book. Even at present she is believed to shower her grace on her devotees. It is significant here to deal with the image-worship especially with respect to *Mother Kālī.* The idol of *Kālī* is an ideal and perfect manifestation and embodiment of the power-element. It involves the mysteries of creation and annihilation which beggar description. According to *Purāṇas* and *Tantras*, there is a mention to eight kinds of idols of *Kālī* out of which especially, Dakṣiṇa Kālī is worshipped in our country. Even in the midst of ten *Mahāvidyās* she holds the first position. She is also called *Ādya Śakti Mahāmāyā* (the primal energy of existence).

The term '*Kālī*' literally refers to black complexion which is also supported by our religious scriptures. She is said to be the most powerful of all the goddesses. She assumes various forms according to the need of hour, i.e., both benign and dreadful. In the benign, she plays positive roles of cultural creativity, bonanza, prosperity, defence, establishment of religious order and material affairs, *Sarasvatī*, *Pārvatī*, *Pṛthvī* and *Mahā Lakṣmī* are the prominent illustrations of the positive one. In

the dreadful, she plays an offensive role. She kills demons and giants and exterminates evils from society. Indeed it is a defensive role in the interest of the cosmos. She pervades from the earth to the sky. She appears dreadful in her countenance but she is large-hearted and merciful. She has four arms which stand for the four objectives of life *Dharma* (righteousness), *Artha* (wealth), *Kāma* (sex), and *Mokṣa* (salvation), the four stages of human life: the first is student stage, the second the married life, the third the recluse life and the fourth the life of complete renunciation.

She wears a girdle of severed hands round her waist. It (the girdle) symbolises involvement and engagement in different types of activities. Her two legs signify heaven and hell, material and immaterial, male and female, knowledge and ignorance, dawn and dusk, day and night. She has dishevelled hair which stands for 'riddance from the flaws of lust and luxury' and also for diversity. She is in the state of nature and lives in the cremation-ground that stands for the human heart. The naked body symbolises the sky and the direction. She stands on the body of *Lard Śiva* who signifies a dead body as his power enters the body from which it emanates. The real meaning of '*Śiva*' is welfare or munificence, which is granted by mother *Kālī* in concrete form for the good of all the creatures of the entire creation. She wears a wreath of skulls which represent the alphabet. "When materialism comes to an end, Spiritualism comes to light" is represented by the benign mother *Kālī* over the chest of Śiva.

MAHĀLAKṢMĪ

It is considered that Mahālakṣmī came into existence in the Vedic period. According to the Ṛgveda, she is called by various names such as Padmamālinī, Aświnī, Ghṛtaśṛ, Daśanśrī etc. On the other hand, according to Purāṇas, she is reputed to be the consort of Viṣṇu. She is the daughter of the ocean. In the other words, she is said to have appeared out of the churning of the oceans by a constellation of gods and demons in order to relish in elixir. Symbolically, the name of mutual attraction and affliction of the ethereal element is the churning of the oceans. The lustre of divine energy is Mahālakṣmī. The water of the oceans is put in comparison with nectar. She is the presiding deity of riches, wealth, bonanza, grace, glory and good fortune. According to Tantraśāstra, she is called Kamālatmika amidst Daśa Mahāvidyās.

She is generally clothed in gold. Sometimes she is seen in a sitting posture and sometimes in a standing one. She has two arms when she is in the company of Viṣṇu. On the other hand, when she is worshipped and prayed to, she is four handed. Her twin hands are graced with the two lotuses which represent a balance and co-ordination between the Soul and the Supreme Being. She is seen pouring down gold coins out of one of her two lower hands. The next one shows a boon-giving pose. She is visibly standing between the two elephants. According to the religious scriptures, she owns a lot of vehicles such as an elephant, an eagle, an owl and a lotus but no doubt, it is the owl which is the vehicle of hers. It is not able to discern in the dim or dazzling light but in the pitch darkness of the night, it sees everything i.e., it is the symbol of tamas (bad tendency) and Yama, the lord of death.

To sum up, so far as her cosmic play is concerned, she has double appearances as Śṛ and Lakṣmī but in reality she is one. The symbolic meaning of Śṛ stands thus:

Ś + R + Ī + (.) Anusvār (it is considered to be dot and a nasal sound).
Ś = Stands for Mahālakṣmī
R for wealth.
Ī for contentment
Anusvār for pain killer and suffering reliever.

MAHĀSARASVATĪ

Mahāsarasvatī is the presiding deity of learning and speech. She is the daughter and consort of Brahmā, the creator. She always remains lustrous in her sweetly graceful as well as white complexioned appearance. She is normally dressed in white. Sometimes her mount is a white coloured swan and sometimes a peacock. In addition, she is also seated on a lotus flower. She has four arms. She presents a lotus or a string of pearls in her hand. In the second, she has a scripture. Sometimes she is seen having a water-pot or vase in her hand, sometimes her hand shows a benediction granting pose. She is seen even playing upon a stringed musical instrument known as Vīṇā which is held by her with her two hands. This is such an instrument as produces a musical and rhythmical note representing the most profound mysteries of the religious scriptures. She is credited with the invention of alphabet.

Mahāsarasvatī's four arms stand for the four directions, four Vedas, four stages of life, four heads of Brahmā, the creator of the four divisions of Dharma, viz. Sādhāraṇa Dharma (universal) Dharma, Veseal Dharma (particular Dharma), Asādhāraṇa Dharma (extraordinary Dharma) and Apaddharma (Dharma under crisis). The scripture is the symbol of spiritual knowledge and motherliness. The wreath stands for alphabet and movement. The peacock represents the art of dance, music, knowledge and force. The swan epitomises non-attachment,

renunciation discretion, purity and soul. The long neck of the swan stands for a profound research into the mysteries of life and creation. The Vīṇā signifies a device which leads us from ignorance to knowledge and enlightenment.

The lotus whereon she is seated is not a physical one but spiritual one. This lotus stands for a thousand-petalled lotus deeply located inside the head. It is worth mentioning in the context of this goddess that schools in India generally begin their activities with the prayer to Sarasvatī. This shows her importance amongst the Indian masses.

GAU MATA
(THE HOLY COW)

There are different types of animals all over the world. Among them a cow (Gau Mata), occupies the most important and valuable place in the Indian psyche. She is the backbone of Indian culture. She is regarded as the most sacred animal in India and its value cannot be denied by any country of the world because her milk has been scientifically proved that it is not only milk but also medicine and ambrosia. According to the religious scriptures, she grants the four objectives of life—*Dharma*, *Artha*, *Kāma* and *Mokṣa*. During the inception of the creation, the Vedas, Agni (fire), a cow and Brahmins came into existence. It is she through whom '*HAVI*' (a special kind of offering to gods and goddesses) is offered to all the deities in yajña which requires certain items—barley, mole, clarified butter, jaggery, etc., that are fulfilled by means of the young ones of a cow namely, a bull. In order to make the altar holy, the cow's urine and dung are essential requirements. She is considered to be a milk goddess who provides milk to the hungry generation. She feeds the hungry, clothes the naked, relieves the patients and supplies an ample quantity of manure, the vital tonic for fields.

The relation between Indian civilization and a cow is inseparable. It is illustrated by an interesting story of *Dilīpa*, the most revered and honourable forefathers of Rāma, the

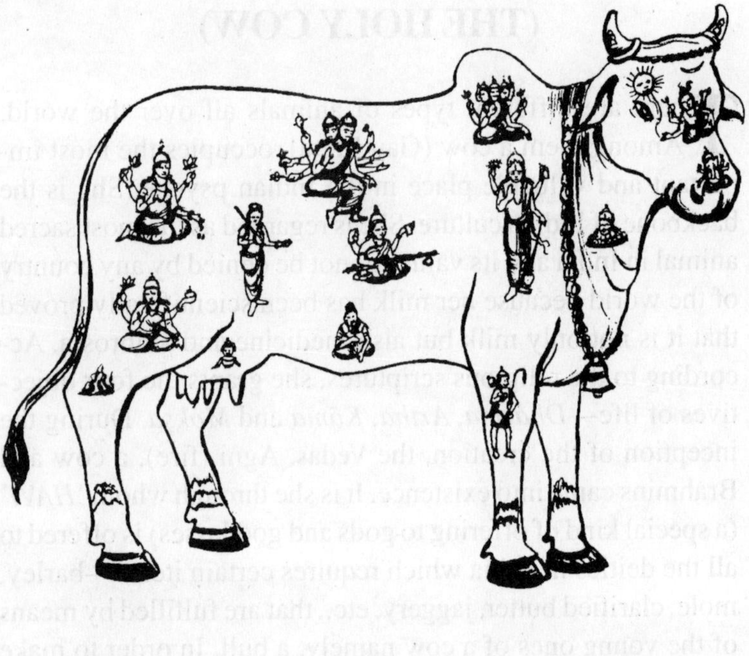

incarnation of Viṣṇu dedicated his life to a fierce and brutal lion for the protection of the cow. Even *Arjun*, in the Mahābhārat period, underwent severe punishment of exile for a span of twelve years to ensure the security and protection of her. *Brahmarṣi, Vaśiṣṭha*, the venerable and great priest of the royal family of *Rāma*, the renowned king of *Ayodhyā*, had a celestial wish-cow known as *Kāmadhenu* which once supplied delicious food and drink in abundance to King *Viśvāmitra* and his retinue who were very hungry, thirsty and tired alter having had a good hunt in a thick jungle of the *Himālayas.*

Remarkably a number of renowned scientists, of the world have already experimented with the cow-dung and urine and drew conclusion succinctly that her milk and urine are extremely effective in lots of diseases like T.B., Jaundice, and Cancer, etc., because they have medicinal properties. They have also much purity.

Though *Śaiva*, *Śāktya*, *Vaiṣṇava*, *Jain*, *Buddha* and *Sikkha* are divided in their opinion with respect to rituals and adoration, all of them pay their respect to the cow. According to the *Mahābhārata, Brahmā, Śiva, Aśvanī Kumār*, the Moon, the Sun, *Pārvatī* constellation, *Lakṣmī*, the Sea, the Sky abide in the different parts of the cow. The tri-world is situated on her back. She possesses *sattva guṇa*, happiness, honesty, light righteousness, to the most possible extent. It is very surprisingly and curiously interesting that *Lakṣmī* belongs to the cow dung and the *Gangā* to urine. It is also notable that the cow dung drives away goblins or ghosts.

The cow represents the greatest amount of miraculous power flowing from the fountain invested with unlimited power.

PṚTHVĪ DEVĪ
(MOTHER EARTH)

Pṛthvī (Earth) finds a gracefully excellent expression in the Hindu mythological scripture as a beautiful daughter of Pṛthu, a great king of his time. She is a paragon of virtue. She pervades everywhere. She is called by different names. Being the issue of Kaśyapa, she bears the name 'Kaśyapi" In the event of being Sthira (stable), she is named of Sthirā. Because of supporting Viśva (the entire world), she is known as Viśvakarmā. Being blessed with ananta rupas (endless forms and shapes), she is called 'Anantā'. On account of having Vasus, she is reputed to be Vasundharā.

The highest souled personage (Mahāvirat Puruṣa) has held the most important position inside the comfortable amount of water since times immemorial. The soft hair on his body metaphorically turns his hermitage (Āśrama from which the earth emanates). At the time of creation, she remains constant on water. On the contrary, at the time of annihilation or Dooms Day, she is immersed in water. She, as a goddess, is surrounded by the seven seas. The seven islands are the parts of her body. She is enriched with the seven paradises, the seven underworlds, the world of the creator (Brahma Loka) and Dhruva Loka.

The complexion of her radiant countenance is like that of a lotus flower. In her appearance, she also looks like full moon day of the autumn season. All the parts of her body are painted with sandal. Different kinds of ornaments add to the beauty of her charming appearance. She treasures countless priceless jewels, that is to say, inside the earth or outside it. She is clothed in pure consciousness. She is found in the role of an observer who maintains the world like an enormous vast family by supporting the animate and inanimate objects, she grants all the creatures not only shelter but also vital force. Millions of devotees worship her. According to Varāha Kalpa, she was in concrete form. For the first time, Hari worshipped her as Varāh. Thereafter all the deities also offered their prayers to her. During the same period of time, Lord Viṣṇu incarnated himself as Varāh. It is not out of place to mention that once upon a time, Lord Viṣṇu liberated her from the cruel hands of the great giant Hiraṇyakṣa by killing him. The Earth presented herself as a consort of Viṣṇu. It was the bright Mars who came into existence by means of the union of both of them. This is the reason that according to astrology, Mars is considered to be the offspring of hers.

PĀRVATĪ

Spiritually, Pārvatī, the dignified goddess, is the primal energy of *Lord Śiva* but as for as the cosmic play by her is concerned (i.e. from the physical point of view), she is his consort. She being the embodiment of meekness and love graced the half part of his body. This way she made him *Arddhanārīśvara*. On the other hand, he was honoured with a suitable title '*Mṛtyuñjaya*'. This credit also goes to her. Remarkably, Pārvatī entered the womb of *Menakā*, the consort of *Himālaya* and at the suitable time she appeared. First of all there arises a question why she is named Pārvatī. In response to it, it can be clearly said that since she was the daughter of *Parvatarāj*, she was reputed to be Parāvatī. When she made up her mind to do severe penance, her mother forbade her to do so. So she came to be known as *Umā*. U + MĀ, 'U' stands for penance and 'Mā' for 'not'. After some time, she stopped eating leaves *(parṇa)* so she became famous as *Aparṇā* (leafless). For the welfare of mankind, she held a certain weapon with which she dispatched *Caṇḍa* and *Muṇḍa*, the two fearsome and formidable demons of the time, so she was known as *Cāmuṇḍā*. She is represented as a fair complexioned deity. All the limbs of her body are well proportioned. Playing the vital role of an ascetic, she did severe penance. It was her Kali's frightening and formidable appearance which aimed at inviting the attention of Śiva when the situation became

increasingly grave and dismal because of giants, demons, and tyrants. As *Gauri*, she pleased him to the most possible extent. She incarnated herself even as *Durgā*.

To sum up, it can be pointed out that she is generally found absorbed in profound meditation holding a rosary (*rudrākṣa*) in one of her hands. Rudra+Akṣa. '*Rudra*' stands for *Lord Śiva* and '*Akṣa*' for the eye. In this way, it is the divine eye-sight that governs and guides the entire world. She always concentrates her mind only on the eye-sight or dynamic power.

RĀDHĀ

Śrī *Rādhā* signifies energy. On analysis, we have two words '*Śrī* and *Rādhā*' *Śrī* = *Ś* + *R* + *Ī* +; *Rādhā* = R + Ā + DH + Ā 'Śrī' means *Lakṣmī* who is the presiding deity of wealth, glory, grandeur, contentment and nourishment: '*Rādhā*' consists of two vowels and two consonants. The vowels represent Brahma, and the consonants represent nature i.e., '*prakṛti*'; and puruṣ. When 'Rā' is pronounced, one becomes free from fault and flaws to the most possible extent in the same way when 'Dhā' is pronounced, the mouth itself open and one gets rid of fault and flaws. In this way both of them supply oxygen that is quite essential for life. Even from the scientific point of view, the process of the opening and closing of the mouth carries much importance because it inhales oxygen but exhales carbon dioxide.

Allegorically and significantly, the mind is filled with the six common human failings which are the sworn enemies of man because they get in the way of achieving the aim of his life. In other words, if the mind is clean like a mirror that is not tainted or soiled with any sense of evil, there will be the clear reflection of an image of 'God'. It is memorable that Śrī Kṛṣṇa is reputed to be lover and connoisseur of sixteen types of works of art. But whatever he has acquired is due to Rādhā only. Just as the force of causticity or inflammation is contained in fire, light and the sun, in the same way, miraculous and mystical power is implied in God. In this way, we would have recourse to *Rādhā* who can help us avoid the failings. It remains inseparable from God. One more glaring instance would be fit to make the aforesaid clearer. Just as a potter is unable to carve out a pitcher without clay, in the like-wise manner, there will be no creation by God without having recourse to Nature.

RATI

'*Rati*' is popularly known as the goddess of passion. She is the consort of Cupid, the god of love. Like her husband, she is the marvellous and living embodiment of beauty and attraction. She has the corpulent body which is of gold colour. Sometimes she is blood coloured like the flower of a pomegranate. She is fair complexioned. She, as a rule, has two hands holding certain weapons that cupid has. Her face wears a gentle smile and she is embellished with different sorts of ornaments.

'*Rati*' is called the presiding deity of beauty, sweetness, sexual intercourse and liveliness. She bears numerous names like '*Prīti*', '*Kāminī*', '*Lalitā*', '*Mahākāriṇī*', '*Kāmeśhī*', '*Kāmapatnī*', '*Manamatha*', '*Manasija Satī*' etc. She abides in the minds of all the creatures just like '*Kāmadeva*'. According to '*Brahmaivarta Purāṇa*', she was born out of the left side of 'Kāmadeva'. In accordance with the Bhāgavata, she emanated from the core of '*Brahmā's*' heart. '*Kalikāpurāṇa*' tells us that she was born out of the sudation of *Dakṣa Prajāpatīs*' body. Remarkably, an oration amorous dalliance, art, song, dance, affection, and posture are the expression of not only Cupid but also of *Rati*. She plays a Significant role with regard to the creation of the world as well as the procreation of different sorts of creatures.

In conformity with the notional creation, when God resolves to open with the coition creation. He manifests himself into two forms which came to be known as '*Cupid*' and '*Passion*' who ceaselessly contribute to the growth and expansion of the vegetables-kingdom and creatures. Really speaking, the lustful attraction and affection between Kāmadeva and Rati is possible by virtue of awareness. But for the amorous dalliance of '*Rati*', there would have been no existence of cohabitation. She possesses the noble and sublime sentiments like beauty, sweetness tenderness, humour, gracefulness dalliance, mirth, etc. Hence, she may be known only through experience and sentiment. It can be added here that if '*Kāmadeva* is endowed with power, *Rati* is its fountain.

SĪTĀ

Sītā is the benign and worthy daughter of the worthy king Janaka who had already identified himself with the Ultimate Reality. She is the consort of Rāma. Sītā is the fountain head of power and Rāma derives power from her. As a matter of fact, there lies no fundamental difference between both of them just as the rays and the sun are inseparable.

According to various scriptures such as the Purāṇas, Vālmīki Rāmāyaṇa, and Hanumāna Nāṭaka etc., with regard to the manifestation of Sītā, there is a mention that once Janaka was ploughing a field and consequently, there was a furrow or a line made of a coulter which gave a gentle blow to a pitcher. Remarkably, it was fraught with blood extracted by demons from the bodies of a host of sages, hermits and gods. The act of cruelty and brutality caused a drought during the reign of the king. It was predicted that if he ploughed the field, there would be a torrential rain. Accordingly, he arrived at a momentous decision as well as translated it into action. As a result, Sītā incarnated herself. Since she was brought up by Janaka, she was named after her father i.e. Janaka Nandinī.

The description of Sītā has it that she possesses broad eyes, tidy hair, a well-shaped nose, strong thighs and a beautiful face like the moon. She is incomparably beautiful. She is renowned throughout the world for her kindness. She is purely gold-complexioned, with her soft and slender waist. She is sprucely garlanded. She has two hands—the first is armed with a lotus flower and the second is graced with a fearless pose. She is unequalled in grace and beauty throughout the world.

The Significance of Sītā:

There three sounds are expressive of her appearance. Sat, Cita and Ānanda are the appearance of hers. She is gifted with Brahmavidyā, the four Vedas, divine glory and enlightenment. All the worlds and gods are not beyond her. The purport of OM, the Almighty (Praṇava), there stands a close relationship between 'Sītā' and 'Auṁ' so far as the power attributes of the two are concerned. The following comparative chart shows these attributes:

AUM	SĪTĀ
A+U+M	S + Ī + T
A for creation	S for creation
U for state or situation	Ī for State or situation
M for Annihilation	T for annihilation

Ī stands for the compendious formula of the mundane affairs or the handiwork of God or Māyā (illusion)

Sītā possesses the three qualities of nature—Sattva, Rajas and Tamas (poise, passion and stupor).

S stands for truth and also for celestial beverage from an ancient creeper and also for nectar.

T stands for something embellished with silver, beauty and a jewel.

It is she who generates, observes and destroys all the animate and inanimate objects. She pervades everywhere for the welfare of gods, mankind and all other creatures.

The real devotion of a devotee is to shelter in the lotus feet of the great Mother Sītā, and to consider himself humble, ignorant, and a sinner. She always blazes the path leading to the material growth as well as spiritual enlightenment either in this world or in the next, suppressing and repressing demoniac bent of mind and displaying the dutifulness of an ideal lady.

The life of Sītā teaches us that in spite of being in difficulties we should not lose patience.

It would be interesting to point out that being gifted with the power of creation, observance and destruction, she does not pose herself. She does not get disheartened in spite of being kidnapped by Rāvaṇa, the demon king of Lanka and also in spite of being separated from Rāma, the incarnation of Viṣṇu.

In this way, she has added to the glory of women folk. She is beyond description even by thousands of the mouths of Śeṣanāga (a mythological serpent supporting the entire earth). Then how can a man find himself capable of extolling her importance?

SVĀHĀ

Svāhā is the energy of ignition and combustibility as well as the consort of Agni Deva, the god of fire. She possesses an extraordinary glowing and radiant personality. Her beauty is beyond words. She appeared from Bhuvaneśvarī, the goddess or the fountain head of the power of totality of all the worlds. She is omnipotent, omniscient, and omnipresent. Her incarnation aims at the good and welfare of mankind as well as a galaxy of gods.

She is called by sixteen names: Svāha, Vahnipriyā, Vahnijāyā, Santoṣakāriṇī, Śakti, Kriyā, Kāladātrī, Paripākakarī, Dhruvā, Gati, Naradāhika, Dahankṣamā, Sansārasārarūpā, Ghorasansāritāriṇī, Deojivanarupā and Deopoṣaṇakāriṇi. After some time, s he became pregnant. Her pregnancy continued for twenty years (from the godly point of view). Hereafter she gave birth to five handsome sons.

Every yajña (holy sacrifice) is performed in the happy presence of the benign goddess Svāhā. In the absence of hers, fire can neither burn anything nor can convey any food used as oblation to the gods.

SVADHĀ

Like Svāhā, Svadhā also holds an important position among all gods and goddesses. She is reputed to be the presiding deity of Śrāddha (the offering of water, food, etc. to the Brāhmins in honour of manes). She possesses in her outstanding qualities of learning and wisdom. She looks like a young ascetic. She is fair complexioned like a jasmine or hundreds of moons. Some parts of her body are graced with gemmed ornaments. She is the incarnation of Goddess Jagadambā's limited power, and always wears a smile on her face. She has all the noble qualities of Lakṣmī. She is seated on a hundred petalled lotus. She is the consort of manes.

She is born, according to the Purāṇas, by the wish of Brahmā not by coition. He created seven manes. Of them four assumed concrete forms and three were the embodiment of radiance. But there was no provision for food-stuff or oblation to them consequently they had to observe fast. So they went to Brahmā and explained their problems to him. Hereafter, in order to solve their problems, he wished a daughter were born and she was born. She was named Svadhā.

Svāhā is used for deities but Svadhā for manes. If Svadhā is pronounced three times, one will enjoy the fruit of Śrāddha, libation of water, oblation. Again one who utters Svadhā, Svāhā three times, i.e. in the morning, noon and evening, is blessed with a beautiful wife and sons.

GAṄGĀ

In the ancient *Āryan* culture the Gaṅgā has been compared to the cow, the *Gita and Gayatri.* The *Gaṅgā* is regarded as the most sacred river of India. As a goddess she is fair complexioned. Her head is gracefully graced with a white crown. She is seated on the back of a crocodile as her vehicle. She has two arms: in one hand, she has a lotus flower and in the other, she holds the lute. According to the *Purāṇas*, she has four arms armed with the four divine items—a vase, a lotus-flower, a fearless pose and a blessing.

According to the *Mahābhārata*, the most precious and valuable treasury of knowledge and enlightenment of the entire world, she is called *'Tripathagāminī*, a river which flows through the three ways. She is called and invoked by different names—*Ida, Nadi, Trīśrota, Tripathagā, Ākāś, Gaṅgā* (galaxy), *Pātāl Gaṅ*gā (a river in the nether) and the Gaṅgā in the world of mortality.

In the post Vedic Period, the Gaṅgā received considerable value and importance. The *Rāmāyaṇa* says that she was born in highly exalted family. Her mother's name was *Manasa* who was consort of the *Himālayas.*

It is remarkable that in Kṛta Yuga (the Golden Age), *Dvāpara Yuga,* (the Silver Age), *Tretā Yuga* (The Copper Age) and *Kali Yuga* (the Iron Age) she is like milk, in *Treta Yuga* like the moon, in *Dvāpara* like sandal and in *Kaliyug* like water. She flows in a crescent manner in *Kāśī.*

The constant and continuous flow of the Gaṅgā conveys to us a message of considerable importance that we should always be active, modest and progressive. She is immensely associated with the Indian culture and interaction and her very flow in this country enriches its cultural variety. She is characterised by joining, combining and coordinating each and every one.

It would be very interesting to mention that it was *Bhagīratha* who managed to propitiate her to descend the earth. Since then, she has been blessing deliverance to all the creatures of the world. The two vases in her two hands represent two types of things–venom and ambrosia, life and death, and creation and annihilation.

THE EXPOSITION OF PLEXUSES (CAKRAS)

THE EXPOSITION OF PLEXUSES (CAKRAS)

The plexuses of Kuṇḍalinī which are of great concern have been graphically described in a highly esteemed and authentic book on yoga entitled Yoga Sūtra which has been originally propounded by *Patañjalī*, an eminent man of letter. It is one of the six schools of Indian philosophy. He has scientifically shed light upon the seven plexuses. The following brief descriptions are presented to shed light on the seven plexuses as proposed by *Patañjalī*:

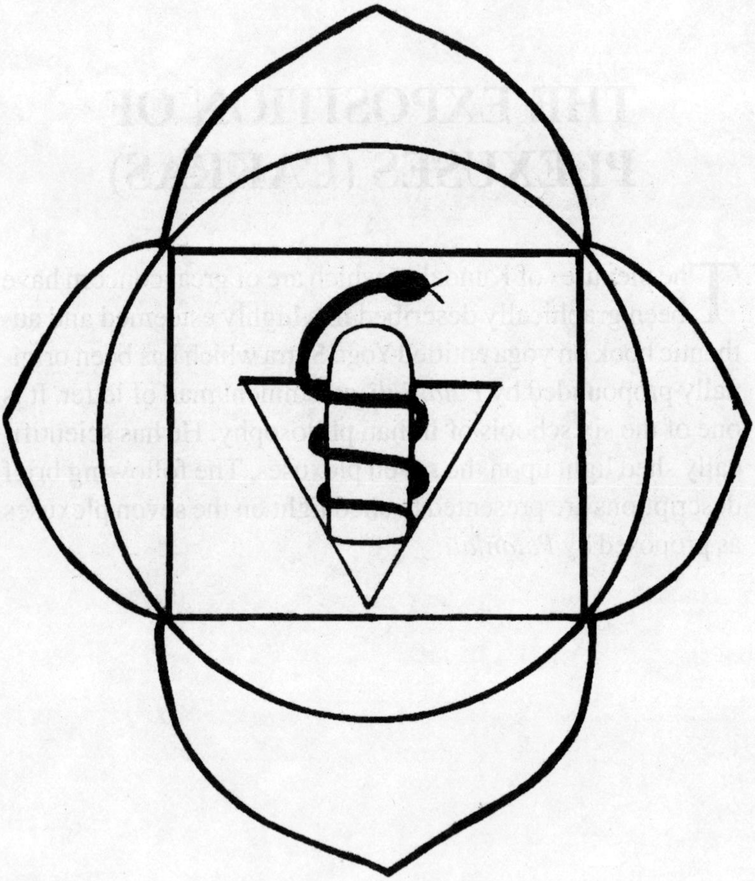

MŪLĀDHĀRA CAKRA (PELVIC PLEXUS)

Kuṇḍalinī, being a manifestly the primal energy, is the pel vic plexus wherein the energy of Kuṇḍalinī is like the recurrence of a conch-shell wrapped in three and a half coil. In the middle of this yoni, there lies a glorious and effulgent blood red basic mantra kliṅ which is static or stagnant air. At its centre, there is self-born phallus in the mouth of Brahma nerve. Significantly one breathes six hundred times in this plexus.

1. The location of plexus: This is located two fingers above the anus and about two fingers below the genitals four. it is just like a power-house that supplies electricity to all the plexuses.

2. Shape: It is compared to a lotus-flower of four petals brightened with the light of blood colour.

3. Attribute: Its intense smell is its dominant quality.

4. Tattva Bīja is 'Lam'.

5. The location of Tattva (element): It is the key location of square and gold coloured earth-element.

6. The letters of petals—There four significant nerves that emanate from this plexus. Pam Śam and Ṣam are written on the four petals of the lotus flower.

7. The location of air—Apān Vāyu (wind form the bowlers) goes downwards.

8. It refers to Bhūlok (the sphere of earth).

9. Action-organ: The anus is designed to discharge excreta or excrement.

10. The Sense-organ—Smell-power is a matter of the nose.

11. The presiding Deity is Ganeśa.

12. The vehicle of Tattva Bīj is Airāvata (God Indra's elephant).

13. Meditation on the plexus yielding a positive result—It is located below the Kānda. It is the junction where there is the confluence of Iḍā, Piṅgalā and Suṣumnā Nāḍīs. Iḍā is also called the Gaṅgā, Suṣumnā is known as the Sarasvatī and Piṅgalā bears the name 'Yamunā'. By fixing one's mind on the plexus, one earns good health, hilarious spirits and prosperity.

SVĀDHIṢṬHĀNA CAKRA
(HYPOGASTRIC PLEXUS)

Svādhiṣṭhāna is located two fingers above the pelvic plexus. In other words, the Hypogastric Plexus is found located inside the Suṣumnā Nāḍī at the root of the reproductory organ. It has control over the lower abdomen and kidneys region. The plexus is of bright red pigment (mercuric sulphide).

This is the particular portion of the body from where six yogic nāḍīs emanate. They look like the petals of a lotus-flower. After experimentation, we come to know that there are certain vibrations which result from the nerves. There is a blatantly clear imprint of letters 'Bam', 'Bham', 'Mam', 'Yam', 'Ram' and 'Lam' on the six petals of the lotus.

The location of the tattva: The region of water is visible at that particular point. The plexus comprises a space like a crescent moon or the form of the conch shell or a particular flower called 'Kunda'. The white coloured Tattva Bīja is Bam. This plexus is of immense concern. It needs concentration as well as it enables us to dispel the element of fear from our mind. Its attribute is rasa. In this plexus, one breathes six thousand times.

MAṆIPURA CAKRA
(EPIGASTRIC PLEXUS OR SOLAR PLEXUS)

Epigastric plexus is located inside the spinal cord facing the navel which is very important and central location from which thousands of nerves emanate and they lead to the four directions and the same number enter the same location. They

form like a network of nerves. The colour of its yantra corresponds to the rising sun. It appears like fire. The vibrations are produced by the nāḍīs. They are represented by the ten letters of Saṁskṛt alphabet: Dam, Dham, Nam, Tam, Tham, Dam, Dham, Nam Pam, and Pham. They are supposed to be imprinted on the ten petals of a lotus. The yantra of this plexus is triangular in form. It is the region of fire, i.e., it is indicated by Agni Tattva, the element of fire. The vehicle of Tattva is a sheep whereon the celestial of fire (Agni Devatā) mounts. This plexus corresponds to svaḥ (the world of paradise). The presiding deity of this plexus is Viṣṇu with four handed Lānkinī. It controls the liver and digestive system. The god and energy of yantra is old Rudra and Lākinī. If one concentrates on this plexus he or she accomplishes pātāla siddhi. We are relieved of ailments and sufferings and do not get afraid of fire. In this plexus, we breath six thousand times.

ANĀHATA CAKRA
(CARDIAC PLEXUS)

Anāhata Cakra is also called 'Hat Cakra' which is located in Suṣumnā nāḍī. This plexus is of deep red complexion and it is Vāyu Tattva the centre of the region of air. Each nerve produces a sound which is represented by the letters that are

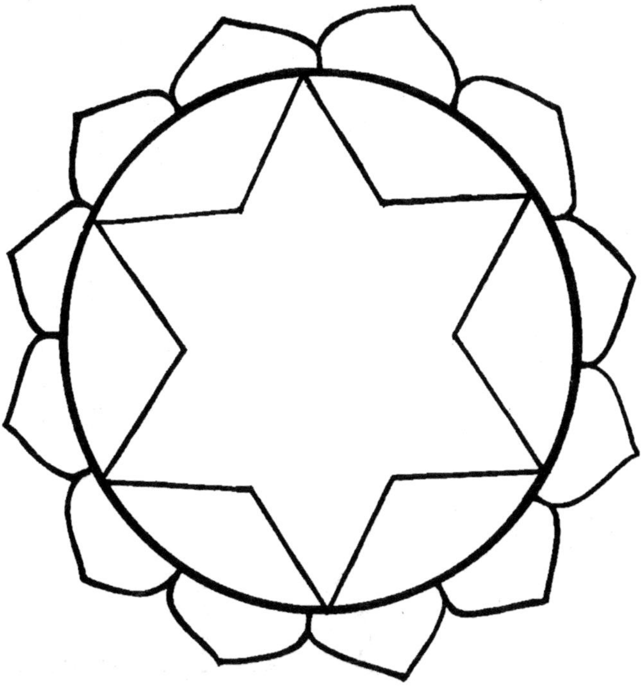

ten in number. They are said to have been imprinted on the twelve petalled lotus flowers. The bījāṅkur 'Yam' is the bīja of vāyu. This plexus has a hexagonal space which is of the hue of collyrum. Its presiding deity is Rudra and god energy is Ḍākinī. The world of this plexus is Maharloka wherefrom Yogic nāḍīs emanate. These are fifteen in number. There is an energy triangle in the middle of this plexus which is the fountain-head of light like electricity. The Cakra has Bana, Lin, Kalp Vṛkṣa is also visible here (a mythological tree which yields anything desired) Anahad Nād (divine melody produced from within) is perceived through the ears. It is also called 'Śabda Brahma'. It is noticeable that one who practices śīrṣāsana for a long span of time, can hear 'Anahad Nād'. The lotus described herein is of eight petals. Its name is Hatpundarika.

Remarkably, the individual soul abides in this plexus. This is why when a practitioner establishes himself herein, he gets identified with the Supreme Being and feels joy unspeakable.

VIŚUDDHA CAKRA
(CAROTID PLEXUS)

Viśuddha Cakra is located inside the Suṣumnā Nāḍī (the spinal column, one of the fourteen nerves of the body) at the base of the throat. Its world is Janaḥ. It is the centre of ethereal element that is of blue pigment. In addition to it, all

other plexuses are associated with 'Mānas Tattva' (mind element which carries much importance and value in human life). In this Cakra, we feel some vibrations that are generated by the nerves. They (vibrations) are shown as 'a', 'ā', i, ī, u, ū, ṛ, Ṛ, ḷ ,Ḷ, e, ai, o, au, aṁ, aḥ. These letters of the Saṁskṛt alphabet are on the sixteen petals of a particular kind which is of smoky-colour. In the Cakra the region of ether is round-shaped. It corresponds to the full moon. Tattva bīja, '*Ham*' which is located at the centre of this plexus. It is called the bīja of Akāla Tattva. It is white complexioned. The vehicle of bīja is an elephant. This yantra (talisman) symbolises the element of ether. On this plexus, one breathes one thousand times.

ĀJÑĀ CAKRA
(MEDULA PLEXUS)

This plexus of white complexion is located inside the Suṣumnā Nāḍī. It is between the eye brows and it has two petals on each side of a lotus-flower. 'Ham' and 'Kṣam' are imprinted on the petals. This plexus consists of Bindu and Śakti. The space between the two petals can be compared to the pineal gland and pituitary body. This Cakra is immensely associated with tap-loka (the world of penance).

The yantra of the plexus induced with the light of electricity is known as 'Itar' which is a phallus of Arddhanārīśvara. Herein the bījākṣara is 'praṇava' (AUM) and the presiding deity is 'Parama Śiva' who lives with his energy Hākinī. This plexus

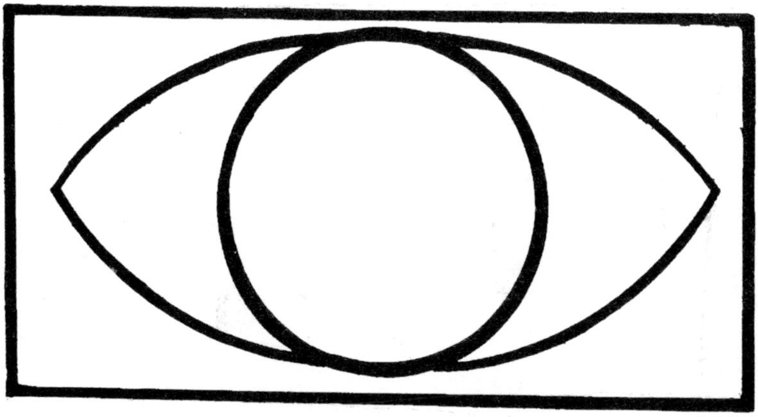

refers to the organ of clairvoyance. If a practitioner establishes oneself inside it (this plexus), a wondrous flame of divine fire comes to the naked eyes. This plexus is known as one induced with the clairvoyance or divine eye. In this stage one is able to perceive each thing which takes place at a considerable distance. Human being is blessed with a divine eye, the third eye of Śiva that is located in the middle of this plexus. By means of this, all the things of the world are achieved by the practitioners. Whatever one thinks, then and there thought are translated into action. All the actions of a previous life come to an end. The practitioner enjoys eight major and thirty two miner accomplishments (Siddhis) which turn then into a liberated soul without disturbing their routine worldly life. On this plexus one breathes one thousand times.

SAHASRĀRA OR ŚŪNYA CAKRA
(CEREBRAL PLEXUS)

This is the plexus which carries major importance. Amidst all the plexuses, the Cerebral Plexus holds a central position. It is called Brahmarandhra and it is of Lord Śiva's

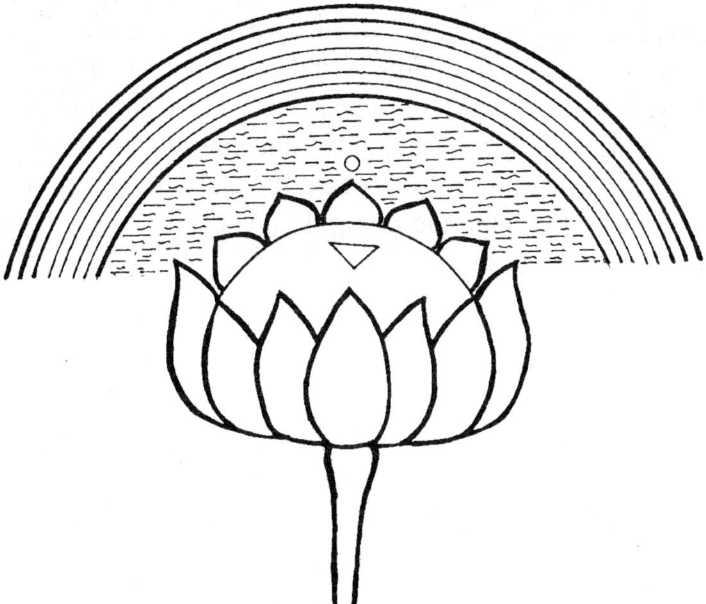

(Svayambhū) abode which is located at the centre of the head. It stands for one thousand petals of a lotus flower though many are divided in their option with respect to the exact figure of petals.

It is noticeable that one thousand yogic nerves proceed from this plexus. The vibrations that are produced by means of the nerves, find expression on the basis of letters of Saṁskṛta (A) to (Kṣa), that is to say, all the vowels and consonants. There is a visibly clear recurrence of these letters on the yogic nerves but they are perceived through the mind's eye, not through the physical eye. It would be very interesting to known that each vowel and consonant is imprinted on its one thousand petals of a lotus flower. The Yantra of the Cakra is the white complexioned full moon. In this plexus Tattva bīja is (:) Visarga 'ḥ' and the presiding deity is Param Brahma (the Great Eternal Spirit) who is with his energy. If a yogi establishes himself or herself in this plexus, he or she realises Him and rises above the physical world. Such a person is never affected by grief or any kind of ailment and does not feel hunger and thirst. The practitioner transcends the cycle of life and death and commands eight (Aṣṭa Siddhis and nine niddhis, eight accomplishments and nine sorts of wealth) and thus one can communes with the Supreme Being. In this plexus one breathes one thousand times.

A PSALM DEDICATED TO THE BENIGN MOTHER

A PSALM DEDICATED TO THE BENIGN MOTHER

Neither I know Mantra
Nor comprehend Yantra
In what fashion to extol
Who pervades the whole
Prayer and profound meditation
Never comes into my attention
Not extremely mighty have I mind
No history of your mystery find
Never I concentrate my mind on ship
That is laden with material of worship
Not feelings in my mind glow
Never tearful looks I show
Your mighty divine pose
Beyond mind always goes
Only your blessing pose
Anti woe give us drug dose
Physically-mentally am I weak
Therefore wish I shelter seek
Human life is fraught with care
Is removed by thy merciful share

(1)

A sinner like me knows not how
To thy bright appearance bow
Herself incarnation of happy liberation
Being bondage know no worshipful adoration
Instantly I am quite out of pocket
Round my neck dangling indolent locket
Countless faults I commit
At last my self son submit
Mother! thou art in the real sense benign
Forgiveness–expression will ever shine
True, a wicked son is possible
But unkind mother is impossible.

(2)

From mother emanating creation
Having no fault with generation
But as far as mine is condition
Terribly am I fickle is indication
Being forsaken mine
Not at all suitable for thine

(3)

Nectar like love-mercy thine
spontaneously flows to mine
To thy service was I cold
Never offered any gold
In each respect am I very mean
But never dim your love-sheen.

(4)

Puzzled by different sorts of work
Deity worship at present I shirk

As am I nearing the sun-set
To me is not open any gate
In this world not have I any hope
Just give me a long hopeful rope

(5)

One who devours the dog's meat
Can start uttering words sweet.
Even the poor with surpassing wealth
Maintain their long time health
A Single letter of a holy utterance
Brings about a miraculous occurrence
How fortunate will be those men
Who are engrossed in chanting with brain

(6)

His cloth is of no doubt sky and direction
Long matted hair gives clear indication
Poisonous snakes round her neck
The Goddess unrivalled him make

(7)

Graced with moon mother bless me
In the core of hear I chant thee.
I do not long for wealth and prosperity
Nor do I desire good luck and liberty

(8)

Adoration not at all on behalf of me
Nor do I know even rituals of thee
Many enormous sins have I committed
Thee with shrill voice have I omitted
A benign Mother like thee
Always show mercy to me

(9)

Today I commit you to memory in distress
As overwhelmed by thirst-hunger I seek your grace
Sorrow and grief has made life brief
So blow to mine your merciful leaf
It is not at all my insincerity
But tr e child's natural quality

(10)

Countless mistakes of small or big size
Goddess is fully merciful not surprise
Crime after crime goes on
Non-the less thy mercy dawn

(11)

O Goddess, none is equal to mine
As far as before my sin is thine
The universe is a vast bower
Where blows energy and power
I am awfully great sinner
But you are great pardoner

ABOUT THE AUTHOR

Born on the first of July 1970 in Buxar, Bihar, Pandit Harendr Upadhyay completed his formal education in 1990. Following in his family tradition Pandit Harendr Upadhyay took up Astrology as his profession. He has practiced Astrology, Palmistry, Phrenology and Tantra-Mantra for the last fifteen years. People from all over India as well as the west have visited his office to consult with him about their various problems related to Astrology, Palmistry and Tantra-Mantra. His interests include solving different problems that are faced by people throughout their lifetimes and reading religious books.

Over the years he has been awarded the *Jyotish Ratna* by the Bharat Dharma Mandal. He has also received testimonials from Anantshree Vibhushit Shrimad Jagadguru Shankeracharya Jyotishpeethadhiswar Shri Swami Swaroopananad Saraswatiji Maharaj and by Dr. Swami Prapannacharya, Member Raj Parishad, Standing Committee Mrigasthali, Kathmandu, Nepal.

The author has also many published articles to his name dealing with Hindu Gods, Goddesses, Tantra and Mantra. As well as his present book he has two others in various stages of completion. The first is ***Sidereal Importance in Human Life***, which deals in depth with Astrology, Palmistry, Phrenology, Numerology, Scar, Muhurata (the auspicious time to start any work), Tantra, Mantra, Yantra, Treatment of bad effects of planets through Astrology, Evil Sprits (Ghosts), Information concerning previous life, How to maintain mental peace and render life prosperous, Rebirth and Architecture (Vastushastra). The second ***A Scientific Approach to Religious Things*** dealing with the concept of Guru, Necessity of Guru, Guru and Discipline, Hermitage (Ashram), Indian Sages and Saints, Ayurveda, Seven Elements in the Human Body, Knowledge of Air and Its place, Six evils of spirituality, Super practice of energy vigil, God is corporal or non-corporal, The practice of Panch Makar, Why image worship? Why are there a hundred and eight beads in a rosary? Rudraksha, suffering, celibacy, pranayama, meditation, devotion pinnacle (sheeka), Sacred thread (Yagyopavit), Spiritual mark (Tilak), Religious sacrifice, Wither does the soul lead after death? Why is a dead body burnt? And Rites after death.

FOR FURTHER INFORMATION

You may contact Pandit Harendr Upadhyay for expert advice in both Western and Eastern traditions of Astrology at the following address.

Tel: 91-542-2314052
email: harendrupadhyay@rediffmail.com
Postal Address
N 15/130-K-1K Sudamapur,
Varanasi, Pin 221010
Uttar Pradesh
INDIA

अशोक